928.70

D1083752

DISCA

Attila the Hun

Other books in the Heroes and Villains series include:

Al Capone
Frederick Douglass
Anne Frank
Genghis Khan
Adolf Hitler
Saddam Hussein
King Arthur
Martin Luther King Jr.
Charles Manson
Josef Mengele
Pol Pot
Oskar Schindler
Joseph Stalin

Heroes and Villains

Attila the Hun

Marilyn Tower Oliver

LUCENT BOOKS

An imprint of Thomson Gale, a part of The Thomson Corporation

THOMSON

GALE

Detroit • New York • San Francisco • San Diego • New Haven, Conn. • Waterville, Maine • London • Munich

To my son Scott, a lover of history.

For more information, contact
Lucent Books
27500 Drake Rd.
Farmington Hills, MI 48331-3535
Or you can visit our Internet site at http://www.gale.com

LIBRARY OF CONGRESS CATALOGING-IN-PUBLICATION DATA

Oliver, Marilyn Tower.
  Attila the Hun / by Marilyn Tower Oliver.
    p. cm. — (Heroes and villains)
Includes bibliographical references and index.
    ISBN 1-59018-638-9 (hbk.: alk. paper)
  1. Attila, d. 453—Juvenile literature. 2. Huns—Biography—Juvenile literature.
3. Huns—History—Juvenile literature. I. Title. II. Series.

D141 045 2005
936'.03'092—dc22

                                                                2005009035

Printed in the United States of America

Contents

Foreword

Good and evil are an ever-present feature of human history. Their presence is reflected through the ages in tales of great heroism and extraordinary villainy. Such tales provide insight into human nature, whether they involve two people or two thousand, for the essence of heroism and villainy is found in deeds rather than in numbers. It is the deeds that pique our interest and lead us to wonder what prompts a man or woman to perform such acts.

Samuel Johnson, the eminent eighteenth-century English writer, once wrote, "The two great movers of the human mind are the desire for good, and fear of evil." The pairing of desire and fear, possibly two of the strongest human emotions, helps explain the intense fascination people have with all things good and evil—and by extension, heroic and villainous.

People are attracted to the person who reaches into a raging river to pull a child from what could have been a watery grave for both, and to the person who risks his or her own life to shepherd hundreds of desperate black slaves to safety on the Underground Railroad. We wonder what qualities these heroes possess that enable them to act against self-interest, and even their own survival. We also wonder if, under similar circumstances, we would behave as they do.

Evil, on the other hand, horrifies as well as intrigues us. Few people can look upon the drifter who mutilates and kills a neighbor or the dictator who presides over the torture and murder of thousands of his own citizens without feeling a sense of revulsion. And yet, as Joseph Conrad writes, we experience "the fascination of the abomination." How else to explain the overwhelming success of a book such as Truman Capote's *In Cold Blood*, which examines in horrifying detail a vicious and senseless murder that took place in the American heartland in the 1960s? The popularity of murder mysteries and Court TV are also evidence of the human fascination with villainy.

Most people recoil in the face of such evil. Yet most feel a deep-seated curiosity about the kind of person who could commit a terrible act. It is perhaps a reflection of our innermost fears that we wonder whether we could resist or stand up to such behavior in our presence or even if we ourselves possess the capacity to commit such terrible crimes.

The Lucent Books Heroes and Villains series capitalizes on our fascination with the perpetrators of both good and evil by introducing readers to some of history's most revered heroes and hated villains. These include heroes such as Frederick Douglass, who knew firsthand the humiliation of slavery and, at great risk to himself, publicly fought to abolish the institution of slavery in America. It also includes villains such as Adolf Hitler, who is remembered both for the devastation of Europe and for the murder of 6 million Jews and thousands of Gypsies, Slavs, and others whom Hitler deemed unworthy of life.

Each book in the Heroes and Villains series examines the life story of a hero or villain from history. Generous use of primary and secondary source quotations gives readers eyewitness views of the life and times of each individual as well as enlivens the narrative. Notes and annotated bibliographies provide stepping-stones to further research.

A Barbarian King

Several years ago when *Time* magazine asked a panel of professional historians to rank the ten most hated persons in history, Attila the Hun, a barbarian king and general who lived during the first half of the fifth century A.D. in what is now Hungary, came in near the top of the list. For centuries in many parts of the world, Attila has been viewed as one of the worst villains in history because of the death and destruction he and his armies brought to much of Europe. Many historians believe that he was a significant factor in the fall of the Roman Empire. Today, sixteen hundred years later, his name remains a synonym for violence and evil. This view of Attila as a villain is not universal, however. In some parts of Europe, notably Hungary, Germany, and Scandinavia, Attila is regarded with respect and in some cases is considered a hero.

There is no question that Attila was a brutal leader who during his short reign brought terror to his enemies and spread fear throughout the formerly all-powerful Roman Empire. In part, he learned his techniques from his ancestors, who in the centuries before his birth had swept across central Asia into Europe, gobbling up territory and terrorizing those they conquered. Hunnic warriors, experts at fighting on horseback, treated their captives without mercy. Such brutal treatment included skinning their captives alive and pressing them to death under heavy boards. Sometimes Huns decorated their belts with the scalps of their victims. The mere mention of their name inspired fear throughout the Roman world.

Attila's actions were also influenced by the period of history in which he lived. The Roman Empire, which had been the most powerful force in the lands surrounding the Mediterranean Sea, had begun to lose control of its outlying territories to barbarian tribes that threatened its borders. In the century before Attila's birth the Visigoths, a Germanic tribe, had attacked and defeated the Roman army at the Battle of Adrianople in the eastern region of the empire, killing forty thousand Roman soldiers. In 410 they attacked and destroyed Rome itself. In the north, another tribe, the Franks, crossed the Rhine River into modern-day France and established a kingdom. The Lombards, another Germanic tribe, controlled part of northern Italy, and the Vandals controlled much of North Africa, formerly part of the Roman Empire. By the time that Attila reached adulthood, Rome was divided into two separate empires governed by weak emperors. The once mighty kingdom was no longer an invincible power.

Sources for Attila's Life

Because the Huns did not have a written language, much of what is known about Attila comes from the writings of Roman and Greek historians who lived in the same era. One of the most important sources was a Greek-speaking Roman historian named Priscus who visited the court of Attila and wrote many descriptions of the leader and his followers. He was the only chronicler who actually met Attila. Although Priscus was influenced by his

Although much of the world has viewed Attila the Hun as a villain, some see him as a hero.

9

The Huns

The Huns were originally nomads from the steppes of central Asia. Their name came from the writings of Chinese historians of the second century B.C. who called them Hsiung-nu, or Eastern Huns. Although their exact origin is unknown, it is believed that they came from Mongolia or perhaps Korea. To keep them from invading their country, in 221 B.C. the Chinese reinforced the Great Wall of China, a 30-foot (9.14 m)-high obstacle that stretched more than 1,500 miles (2,414 km) along China's northern border.

Starting in the beginning of the third century A.D., the Huns swept across central Asia, conquering all who got in their way and cutting a swath of terror. By the middle of the 370s they had crossed the Volga River in what is today Russia. Then they turned toward the territories controlled by the Eastern Roman Empire, where they clashed with Germanic and Persian tribes. By 406 they had crossed the Rhine River into the territories of the Germanic tribes.

The Huns' brutal method of fighting and their wild appearance caused terror and fear. In his book *Barbarian Europe*, British author Philip Dixon writes of the Huns: "They were identified as the Horsemen of the Apocalypse, as Magog, as the offspring of devils who overcame their enemies by magic. More prosaically, but no more accurately, they were identified with the long-vanished tribes of the far north, the Scythians, Cimmerians or Massagetae, and it was asserted that they ate no cooked food, drank blood, lived and slept on their horses, and were so ugly one would think them two legged beasts.' The Roman army,' said St. Jerome, 'is terrified by the very sight of them.' The language they spoke survives only in the form of personal names .... Very little is known of their history before they reached the fringes of the Roman world in the 370s."

Roman viewpoint, which regarded the Huns as barbarians, he was impressed by Attila's leadership abilities. Another source was the Goth historian Jordanes, who was present at many of the battles between the Huns and the Romans that took place in what is today France, Germany, and Italy.

The descriptions of these writers give insight into the life and times of Attila, but their writings also show a bias toward the Roman point of view, which considered the Huns uncivilized barbarians and Attila as their villainous leader. This opinion continued through much of Western history. Hungarians view Attila from a different perspective, however. For them, he is a national hero who personified courage and leadership. In Hungary, Attila is still a popular name for boys. The Germans also have a positive view of Attila, who is portrayed in their mythology as a noble ruler. In the twelfth-century epic the "Song of the Nibelungs," Attila is known as Etzel, a peaceful medieval king.

Although the scarcity of original source materials regarding the facts of Attila's reign is responsible in part for the diversity of viewpoints surrounding his life, his actions have caused his rep-utation to grow throughout the centuries following his death. Attila's deeds have fascinated writers throughout Western history. His life has been de-picted in dramas, films, and opera, where he is usually portrayed as a vil-lain. His name still brings forth visions of bloodshed and violence. For many he remains one of the most infamous, vi-cious leaders in history.

Chapter One

PREPARATION FOR LEADERSHIP

During the first thirty years of Attila's life there was little evidence of the violent and brutal reputation he would later earn during his eight-year reign. Although there are limited sources about his earliest years, those that exist suggest that he was being groomed to take a leadership role in the Huns' military and political life. These years coincided with a period of transition for the Huns, who were abandoning their nomadic lifestyle and becoming an important military force on the borders of the Roman Empire.

Attila's People, the Huns

Attila's people, the Huns, were fierce barbarian nomads whose origins are unclear, although many historians believe that they probably originated in Mongolia. During the two hundred years before Attila's birth, they had gradually swept across central Asia into Europe, spreading death and destruction wherever they went. Lacking an economy based on trade or agriculture, the Huns' principal means of acquiring wealth was forcing those they conquered to pay them tributes, or protection money, to avoid further devastation. Although they were racially and culturally related, the various Hunnic tribes were not yet united into a single force.

A few decades before Attila's birth, the group of Hunnic tribes that were led by his family defeated a Roman force in central Europe in an area around the Danube River; by A.D. 400 they controlled an area that extended from the Caspian Sea to what is today Hungary. The Romans called this territory Pannonia. The Huns had traditionally lived a nomadic lifestyle, but by the late fourth century they had begun to settle in a primitive community located on the banks of a branch of the Danube near the modern-day Hungarian city Szeged. The settlement was probably composed of a vast encampment of chariots and wagons in which families lived and a few wooden structures serving as homes for the leaders.

Attila's Birth and Family

Historians believe that Attila was born in this community sometime between 395 and 406. French historian Marcel Brion writes, "The infant was given the name of Attila which in the Huns' language meant 'Little father,' and perhaps

because this name [Atil] was also what they called the Volga, the river his father greatly admired."[1] Other scholars of the Huns' language believe that the name meant "iron" and designated the strength and leadership that seers predicted for the young child.

Attila's infancy would have been harsh. At times, he might not have received much to eat to teach him how to survive the hardship that was part of the Huns' nomadic lifestyle. Like other young male babies in the Hunnic culture, Attila's cheeks may have been cut with a sword to teach him how to endure pain. In addition, his face might have been flattened to make it possible for him to later wear the helmet worn

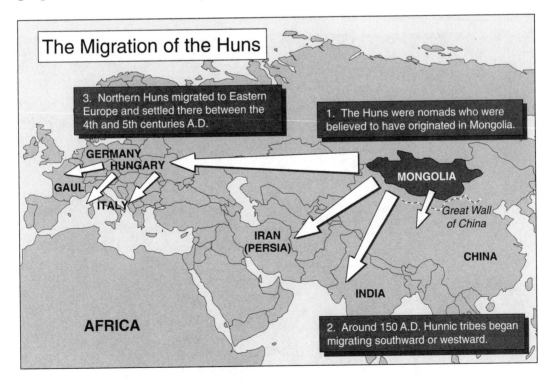

The Migration of the Huns

3. Northern Huns migrated to Eastern Europe and settled there between the 4th and 5th centuries A.D.

1. The Huns were nomads who were believed to have originated in Mongolia.

GERMANY
HUNGARY
GAUL
ITALY
MONGOLIA
Great Wall of China
IRAN (PERSIA)
CHINA
INDIA
AFRICA

2. Around 150 A.D. Hunnic tribes began migrating southward or westward.

by Hunnic warriors. The third-century Roman writer Sidonius Apollinaris described how the faces of Hun boys were disfigured: "The nostrils, while soft, are blunted by an encircling band to prevent the two passages (the nose) from growing outward between the cheekbones, that thus they make room for the helmets; for these children are born for battles, and a mother's love disfigures them."[2]

Attila's family was powerful. His father was Mundzuk, a warrior who was second in command over the Hun military forces that were led by his brother King Ruga. A third brother, Octar, also held a position of leadership. The identity of Attila's mother is unknown. His family probably included several related families who made up a clan. Because it was a common practice for a man to have more than one wife, Attila likely had several brothers and sisters, but the identity of only one, his older brother Bleda, is known.

The Education of a Young Boy in Hunnic Culture

Not long after Attila's birth, his father died, and his uncles took over the task of raising their nephew to be a Hunnic warrior. Because the Huns depended heavily on their military power, a young boy's training as a soldier required learning the arts of horsemanship and

The Huns were trained to be warriors. From early childhood, Attila was taught to endure hardship and pain as training for a warrior's life.

warfare at an early age. Before Attila reached the age of five, he was trained to ride a horse. Perhaps his first lessons in sitting astride an animal involved having him ride on the back of a sheep. When his legs had developed sufficient strength, he would have been given a horse of his own to ride. His lessons would have included archery, fencing with a sword, lance throwing, and the use of a lasso to entangle enemies so they could not continue to fight. To practice these skills, he also took part in mock battles and war games.

Because war and fighting were an integral part of the Huns' culture, as soon as a young boy was able to fight, he was expected to take part in raids on neighboring villages. As Attila's skills improved, he would have been taken on longer military attacks against weaker adversaries. From these forays he apparently learned to enjoy brutality. Marcel Brion writes, "The terror of the people that the Huns pursued taught him to enjoy force and have contempt for weakness."[3]

In addition to learning military skills, Attila was told stories about the history and legends of the Huns. He was also taught about their religion, which was a type of nature worship that relied on shamans or priests who acted as intermediaries between the human and supernatural worlds. The shamans predicted the future by examining the entrails and bones of cattle and sheep, a practice known as scapulimancy. Because the Huns did not have a written language, Attila did not learn to read and write.

During these early years, Attila became immersed in the culture and lifestyle of the Huns, but other than his participation in raids against nearby towns and villages, he learned little about the world outside the Huns' territory. When Attila was about nine years old, however, the introduction of a young hostage named Aëtius gave him a glimpse into the ways of another powerful people, the Romans.

An Exchange of Hostages

During the years that the Huns had been spreading their influence through central Europe, the Roman Empire, which controlled a vast territory that extended from the Mediterranean through eastern and western Europe, had been gradually weakening. In the fourth century the empire had split into two parts—the eastern empire, based in Constantinople (present-day Istanbul, Turkey), and the western empire, based in Italy with Ravenna as its capital. Although the two empires were ruled separately by their own emperors, they were still closely allied, both politically and through family ties.

As the Huns had moved westward in their search for new territories to control, they had displaced other barbarian tribes who had taken up residence along the borders of the Roman lands. Because the Romans feared losing territory to these barbarians, they sometimes formed alliances with the

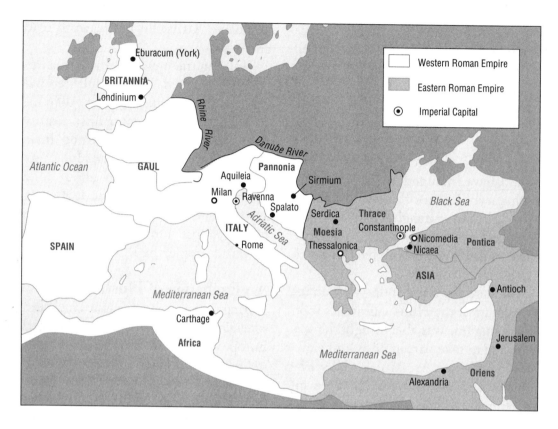

Huns, whom they hired as mercenary soldiers to fight the barbarians alongside the Roman army.

Between 405 and 409, the Western Roman Empire found itself under periodic attacks from a Germanic barbarian tribe called the Visigoths, or Western Goths, whose king was named Alaric. Because their forces were not as strong as those of the Visigoths, the Romans turned to the group of Huns led by Attila's family for help in the form of hired soldiers. Sometime during this period a young Roman noble named Flavius Aëtius was sent to live with the Huns as a hostage to guarantee that the Romans would keep their promises to the Huns regarding payment for the soldiers and other matters. The exchange of hostages was a long-standing tradition of the Romans and groups that opposed them.

Aëtius was a few years older than Attila, but the two became friends. While Aëtius learned the Hunnic language and observed the Huns' lifestyle, Attila took advantage of the friendship to learn Latin, the language of the Romans. This skill proved useful, for a few years later Ruga sent Attila to Ravenna as a hostage. At the time, he was probably eleven or twelve years old. It is possible that Ruga chose him as a hostage, rather than his older brother Bleda, because Ruga sensed that Attila could be a possible rival for power. Brion writes, "His uncle preferred his nephew Bleda, who had a docile character that lacked ambition. He thought the Roman court would soften or break the precocious boy [Attila]."[4]

Attila's Life Among the Romans

When Attila arrived in Ravenna, he found the lifestyle and culture very different from the simple ways of the Huns. Whereas personal cleanliness was not important to the Huns, the Romans had baths built into their homes. The Huns' clothing was worn until it fell apart, while the Romans wore clean clothing. The Romans' rich foods also contrasted with the simple diet of the Huns, which often consisted of raw meat.

Attila found it difficult to adjust to life in the Roman capital. Brion explains:

The Divided Roman Empire

During the last two centuries of its existence, the Roman Empire, which at one time had controlled much of Europe and the Middle East, was in a state of decline. In the late fourth century, the empire split into two factions. The split was caused by corrupt leadership, a changing economy, and the gradual rise of Christianity as a major religion in parts of the empire.

After becoming emperor, Constantine the Great had converted to Christianity and moved the capital of the empire from Rome to Byzantium, a town on the Black Sea that he renamed Constantinople. Today, it is known as Istanbul, Turkey. After Constantine's death in 337 his empire was ruled by three of his sons.

By 352, bickering between various factions of the ruling family brought about a rift, and the western territories, based in Italy, broke away, creating two separate empires. During the latter part of the century the capital city of Rome had lost much of its former splendor. In 402, the Western Romans moved their capital to Ravenna, a town in northern Italy. Of the two empires, the western empire was the most vulnerable to attacks from barbarian tribes.

As the Huns had moved across eastern Europe, conquering various barbarian tribes, these tribes relocated closer to the Roman Empire, threatening the Romans' authority. To keep the barbarian tribes under control, the Romans paid money, called tribute, to their leaders. As long as the payment was made, the Romans believed they would be free from attack. This tactic was not always effective. In 410 the Visigoths, a barbarian tribe led by King Alaric, overran much of Italy and plundered Rome.

Brusquely transported from the Danube valley to the Roman Empire, Attila was like a caged beast. He suffocated in the perfumed halls. The luxury which dazzled other hostages, disgusted him. . . . He remembered his wooden home at the edge of the river and the leather tents of his people. Accustomed to drinking mare's milk and eating raw meat, he spit on the offerings of the Roman cooks. Everything in the sumptuous home where he felt like a prisoner oppressed and wounded him. . . . He hid his anger and his disgust.[5]

Attila observed signs of decay in the luxurious Roman lifestyle. By the fifth century, the western empire was slipping into a decline caused by corrupt leadership, a failing economic system that overtaxed its citizens, and a breakdown of law and order. He also noticed that while many people lived in poverty, the Roman elite enjoyed a lavish lifestyle and decadent pastimes such as spectacles that pitted men against animals who tore them to pieces.

Even though Attila was unimpressed by the Roman way of life, he took advantage of his time as a hostage to improve his Latin and learn Greek, the official languages of the eastern and western empires. It is believed that his stay in Ravenna and all that he observed there inspired in him not only a desire to ultimately conquer the Romans but the con-

The Romans built baths such as this to maintain health and civility. Attila found such luxuries disgusting and decadent.

Hostages

The custom of taking hostages, individuals who are held under the control of a hostile or enemy power as a guarantee that certain promises be kept, has an ancient history. Usually, the person taken hostage is a civilian and not a member of a military force. The hostage's situation differs from that of a prisoner of war in that his or her safety depends on the fulfillment of certain demands and conditions. Usually, the hostage is used as a bargaining tool to force an opposing power to make concessions it might not otherwise agree to.

One of the earliest known incidents involving hostages occurred during the reign of the Egyptian king Thutmose III (1469–1426 B.C.), considered by many the greatest of all Egyptian pharaohs. He established a system in which native rulers he conquered paid a yearly tribute to Egypt and sent their sons as hostages to be educated at the court. In this case, the hostages helped guarantee peace between Egypt and the native tribes, and the young men learned the traditions and language of a new culture.

The Romans took young men as hostages as early as 189 B.C. when Antiochus III, the son of the king of Syria, was taken as a hostage to Rome, where he learned Roman customs and traditions. After his release, he conquered most of Egypt and ruled there as regent for his nephew Ptolemy VI.

viction that this was a possible goal. According to Brion, "He would keep names and information in his memory for later use. The Romans may have scoffed at the brutal character of the young boy, but they did not sense the potential of his hatred, and his knowledge of their weaknesses and their defaults. Hidden inside his hard and rigid will was a certainty of future triumph."[6]

A few years later, when his time as a hostage was up, Attila was apparently happy to return to the simpler, more severe lifestyle of his own people in Pannonia. The date of his return is unknown.

The Huns from 410 to 420

The period of political history of the Huns and events of Attila's life between 410 and 420 are relatively unknown because the work of the only writer of this period, a Constantinople scholar named Olympiodorus, has been lost. Historians believe that at this time there was still no united Hun force but, rather, various clusters of tribes who lived in scattered territories in what is today Romania, Yugoslavia, Hungary, and parts of Russia.

During this period Attila's uncles, Octar and Ruga, jointly ruled over the tribes of Huns living in central Europe. Their division of power is unclear to scholars, but historian Otto J. Maenchen-Helfen suggests that the two may have had jurisdiction over separate areas. He writes, "Octar had nothing to do with the East Romans, whose only enemy was Ruga."[7]

It is believed that by 420 Attila and Bleda had also assumed leadership roles in the Hunnic military force. During this time, Attila also married a woman named Kreka, the first of his many wives. Meanwhile, mounting tensions in the Roman Empire created circumstances that would prove advantageous to the Huns, who received gold for their service as mercenary soldiers hired by the Romans.

Upheaval in the Western Roman Empire

Between 410 and 423 political unrest in the Western Roman Empire led to confrontations between various factions seeking control of the government. Constantius III, coemperor with Honorius, died. Afterward, his widow, Galla Placidia, who was Honorius's sister, was accused of plotting against her brother for power. To save her life and that of Valentinian, her young son who was an heir to the throne, she fled to Constantinople, where her nephew, Theodosius II, was emperor of the Eastern Roman Empire.

When Honorius died later that year, a high Roman official named John proclaimed himself emperor over the western empire. Because many people objected to his rule, civil war broke out in Italy. To help stabilize the situation, John sent Aëtius, now an official in the court, to Pannonia to recruit an army of sixty thousand men. Attila had a leadership role in this army.

Although Aëtius's previous friendship with Attila and his knowledge about the Huns may have been a small factor in their agreeing to fight for him, the principal reason for the Huns' support was greed. Maenchen-Helfen writes, "They [Huns] sent their horsemen to Italy not out of friendship with Aetius but because they were paid a great sum of gold. . . . It is almost certain that they were promised regular annual tributes."[8]

Even though the Huns arrived three days after John was executed by forces sent by Galla Placidia, who hoped to regain the throne for her son, they still received the promised gold before returning home. Aëtius made a tentative peace with Galla Placidia, who installed the six-year-old Valentinian as emperor of the western empire. Because of Aëtius's support for the usurper, however, he lost his position in the Roman court and was banished to Gaul (present-day France).

Attila gained much experience during the Roman military campaign and others led by Ruga. Seeing the tribute of gold that the Romans paid to the Huns for their participation in battle gave him a taste for wealth. His experiences in all of Ruga's campaigns during the 420s also helped him hone his skills as a military and political leader.

A Roman coin bears the image of Galla Placidia, empress of the western empire.

Although the Huns had lived up to their reputation as formidable warriors, in the 420s they were still not unified as a single people with a homeland of their own. Ruga could bring together men from diverse tribes of Huns and allied barbarians to fight as mercenary soldiers, but after a conflict ended, they returned to their own tribal territories. Those Huns who owed direct allegiance to Ruga returned to their families in Pannonia.

The Romans Cede a Portion of Pannonia

Even though the Huns had lived in the territories known as Pannonia for approximately fifty years, the land was still officially part of the Roman Empire.

Around 427, for reasons not understood by historians, the Romans attacked the Huns and won a portion of the territory back. Historical sources are unclear about how much territory was involved, but the Huns' loss points to a weakening of their leaders' ability to hold together the confederation that two years earlier had been able to send a huge army to fight in Italy.

In 432 Aëtius, who had been living on his estate in Gaul, feared that his enemies were plotting to assassinate him. Wanting to regain his power and influence in the Roman court, he sought support from the Huns. According to Maenchen-Helfen, "When some of his enemies by an unexpected attack attempted to seize him, he [Aëtius] fled to Rome, and from there to Dalmatia. By way of Pannonia, he reached the Huns. Through their friendship and help he obtained peace with the rulers and was reinstated in his old office."[9] To reward the Huns for their assistance, Aëtius negotiated a treaty in 433 that ceded a portion of Pannonia to them. Author Patrick Howarth writes: "For Ruga this was a considerable diplomatic triumph. The Huns, for so long a nomadic people, now had a permanent home, a change which clearly affected their lifestyle and culture."[10]

The Death of Ruga and a Change in Leadership

In 433–434 while the Huns were preparing to attack the Balkan territories belonging to the Eastern Roman Empire, Ruga unexpectedly died. Scholars argue

Flavius Aëtius

The Roman Flavius Aëtius played an important role in Attila's life. Aëtius was the son of Gaudentius, who may have been a barbarian who rose to importance in the western empire. As a youth, Aëtius spent time as a hostage with both the Goths and the Huns. This gave him knowledge of the culture and fighting techniques of these two potential enemies of Rome.

In 425 Aëtius led an army of sixty thousand barbarians, most of whom were Huns, into Italy to support a usurper named John who had proclaimed himself emperor. Later, when John was defeated, Aëtius persuaded Galla Placidia, the empress, to make him the master of soldiers in Gaul, where he earned a reputation as a superb military man. From 433 to 450, he was a dominant figure in the western empire, and in 451 he challenged Attila at the Battle of Châlons, defeating his old friend.

Because of his strong leadership abilities, he was a threat to the weak Roman emperor Valentinian, who used his skills but distrusted his motivations, believing that Aëtius had his eye on the throne. When Aëtius presented himself at court to claim the emperor's daughter in marriage for his son, Valentinian killed him. Aëtius is still known as one of the most valiant military men in the later years of the Roman Empire.

about the exact date and cause of his death, but according to the Christian historian Socrates Scholasticus, Ruga was struck by lightning while on the battlefield. Although Ruga had a surviving brother, Oebarsius, the leadership of the Huns passed to his nephews, Bleda and Attila, who had proved their courage and ability to lead. Scholars believe that, of the two, Bleda had the greater authority at first. Howarth writes, "Attila was a powerful prince, enjoying considerable independence, but his status was that of second-in-command."[11]

Attila was now in his thirties. Although he had apparently taken part in a number of campaigns as a military leader, up to this point he had not yet experienced the challenge of leadership on his own. His early experiences, however, had given him valuable firsthand knowledge of the Romans' culture and language. He also was ambitious. Author Marcel Brion notes that Attila possessed patience and the ability to wait until a favorable time to assert his authority: "He did not try to intervene in the politics of Ruga. . . . Without impatience, without anger, he waited. He had the confidence of his destiny . . . until the day came for him to realize his goals."[12]

Chapter Two

Attila Takes on the Role of Leader

During the next eleven years Attila worked to establish his position as primary leader of the Huns. Although at first the responsibilities of leadership were divided between Attila and his brother Bleda, Attila was not a person who could easily share authority. During the years of their joint rule, Attila's actions gradually contributed to his reputation as the stronger leader of the two. The challenges he faced were bringing the diverse nomadic tribes of Huns into the federation ruled by his family and forcing the eastern Romans to acknowledge the Huns' military authority over parts of their outlying territories.

The Brothers Take Control

Following the death of Ruga, Attila and Bleda undertook the job of consolidating their leadership. The territories they had inherited consisted of a loose confederation made up of Hunnic tribes and other allied barbarians in central Europe who had owed allegiance to Ruga. It appears, however, that the confederation lacked strength and unity. Patrick Howarth writes, "The consolidation of the various tribes into a single kingdom was a gradual process, which had probably not been completed in Ruga's time."[13] Outside the confederation were other tribes of Huns living in Russia and central Asia. These tribes shared a common language and tradition but operated as independent groups with little or no connection to the Huns living in Pannonia.

During these first years of their coleadership of the Huns, Attila, as the younger son, was second in importance to his older brother. The personalities of the two brothers were apparently quite different. Attila had a rather moody and serious personality; Bleda was a more boisterous man. Nevertheless, at first the two brothers worked well together. Despite his status as older brother and his somewhat greater power among the Huns, Bleda conferred often with Attila, and most decisions, especially in matters of foreign policy, were made by the brothers jointly. As time went by,

Theodosius II, emperor of the Eastern Roman Empire, negotiated a peace treaty with Attila and Bleda at Margus.

however, Attila emerged as the more dominant of the two.

At first, Attila and Bleda divided Pannonia into two regions. The historian E.A. Thompson writes, "Although the two brothers always acted in concert, so far as we know, and regarded their empire as a single property, they divided it between them and ruled separately; but we do not know which portion was allotted to each."[14] It is believed by some scholars that Attila became the leader of the southern section of the kingdom, where he would have his first taste as ruler in his own right.

One of the first challenges Attila and Bleda faced was dealing with the Eastern Roman Empire, ruled by the emperor Theodosius II. The Huns were a more powerful military force than the eastern Romans, and they wanted to maintain this advantage. They also wanted to continue receiving an annual tribute of 350 pounds of gold, an amount the eastern Romans had agreed to pay Ruga in order to maintain peace with the Huns. When Theodosius learned of Ruga's death, he decided to stop the annual payment, perhaps believing that negotiations with the two inexperienced leaders would be easier than they had been with their uncle. Bleda and Attila, however, thought differently, and they demanded a meeting to negotiate new terms.

The Peace of Margus

The two sides agreed to meet in the city of Margus, an important trading center

Emperor Theodosius II

When Arcadius, emperor of the Eastern Roman Empire, died in 408, his young son, a boy of six, succeeded him as Theodosius II. Because of his young age, his older sister, Pulcheria, took over the government in his name. During his youth, he would sign his name to documents of state that were drawn up by administrators, who were the powers behind the throne.

Later in life, he was still controlled by these administrators, especially by one named Chrysaphius. A contemporary historian, John of Antioch, described the influence of these advisers on Theodosius as quoted in Colin Douglas Gordon's *Age of Attila*. He wrote: "Theodosius received his office from his father, and because he was unwarlike, lived in cowardice, and won peace by money not arms. He brought many evils on the Roman state. Having been brought up under the influence of [administrators], he was well disposed to their every command."

From the 420s to Theodosius's death in 450, his empire was challenged by the Huns, who periodically mounted raids to grab territory and demand tribute. Because he was a weak ruler, Theodosius was often at a disadvantage in his negotiations with the Huns. One of his lasting accomplishments, however, was the construction of massive walls around Constantinople to defend the city from Attila's forces. Many of these fortifications still stand today.

in the Balkans, located at a juncture of the Danube and Morava rivers in what today is Serbia. To show his good faith, Theodosius sent two of his most important diplomats, Plinthas and Epigenes, to negotiate with Bleda and Attila, who pitched their lavishly decorated tents across from the Roman compound.

Although the Romans were more sophisticated than the Huns, the two brothers managed to outsmart them. When Attila and Bleda arrived at the meeting, they refused to dismount from their horses. The Romans, accustomed to a more formal style of negotiating, were taken by surprise. If they dismounted, they would have to look up to the mounted Huns, which would make them appear weaker; thus, the Romans were forced to remain on horseback in order to preserve their dignity. The tactic was a shrewd psychological move that reminded the Romans of the Huns' superior horsemanship and the devastation that might result if Attila and Bleda decided to attack the Romans. Because the Romans were unaccustomed to negotiating under these conditions and they feared what might happen if they did not concede, the agreements made were to the advantage of the Huns.

One issue at stake was the return of barbarian fugitives who had fled to the eastern empire from lands taken over by the Huns. Some had done so to escape brutal treatment by the Huns under Bleda and Attila; others preferred to fight for the Romans as mercenaries rather than live under Hunnic control. Also among the fugitives were Huns who had deserted their own tribes to live under the protection of the Romans.

Attila and Bleda considered the return of these fugitives important to the Huns' security because they did not want them fighting on the side of the eastern Romans. The Romans were forced to agree that they would not accept any more escapees and that they would begin extraditing the remaining fugitives living under their jurisdiction. The Romans also agreed that they would not ally

Fugitives from the Huns and other barbarian tribes who had asylum in the Roman Empire would be forced to return to Hunnic lands as part of the Peace of Margus.

themselves with any groups the Huns were fighting against. Trading rights were at stake as well. The Huns demanded that they be allowed to trade on equal terms with Roman merchants along the borders between Hunnic and Roman lands. Finally, Attila and Bleda insisted that the Romans pay the Huns an annual tribute of seven hundred pounds of gold, twice the sum that had been demanded by Ruga.

The Romans agreed to these terms in a treaty called the Peace of Margus, which was signed in 435 and proved to be a triumph for the new Hun leaders. It is not known which of the brothers took a more dominant role in the negotiations, but some historians believe that Attila took the lead. According to Marcel Brion, "The ambassadors were . . . intimidated by Attila's majesty and his intransigence, and they did not dare to refuse. There was within this small, squat man a sort of noble wildness that imposed respect and fear."[15] At any rate, shrewd maneuvering had enabled Attila and Bleda to obtain a conquest without shedding a drop of Hunnic blood.

Initially, the Romans kept the terms of the agreement by returning some of the barbarians who had sought refuge in the Eastern Roman Empire. Among those sent back were two young boys named Mama and Atakam, who were from a royal clan related to the Huns. Attila and Bleda responded violently. When the boys arrived in Hunnic territory, they were crucified as punishment for their es-cape to the Romans and to serve as a warning to others who might seek refuge in Constantinople. In one short year of rule, Attila and Bleda had managed to re-inforce the Huns' reputation for viciousness in battle, cleverness in negotiation, and vengefulness against those who attempted to oppose their drive for power.

Attila and Bleda Expand Their Territories

For the next few years, relative peace existed between the Huns and the eastern Romans, allowing Bleda and Attila to turn their attention toward expanding their empire in other directions. By attacking and conquering tribes of Germans, Slavs, and Turks who lived along their northwestern and eastern borders, they were able to extend their rule over an area that included the Caucasus Mountains to the east.

Although a majority of Huns eventually established settlements around the Danube River, where they came under the control of Attila and Bleda, some tribes remained separate. Among these was a group known as the White Huns, who lived in an area of Russia along the northern frontier with Persia (present-day Iran). The sixth-century Byzantine writer Procopius wrote of the White Huns, "They do not mingle with any of the Huns known to us, for they occupy a land neither adjoining nor even very near to them."[16]

One of Attila's major accomplishments during this period was bringing

The Payment of Tribute

One of the principal sources of wealth for the Huns was the gold that they demanded as tribute from the Romans. This payment served as a guarantee that the barbarians would not attack the Roman outposts. In the 440s the eastern Romans paid the Huns about thirteen thousand pounds of gold. In 447 the payment of six thousand pounds of gold was a particularly heavy blow to the imperial treasury, requiring the government to levy a large tax on its citizens to raise the necessary funds.

The Huns were not the only barbarian tribe to demand tribute from the Romans. In 408 Alaric, the Visigoth leader, demanded four thousand pounds of gold from the western Romans. Later that year, his troops blockaded Rome, and the Romans paid him five thousand pounds of gold and thirty thousand pounds of silver to leave.

The Roman money of the time was called *solidi*. The Huns, fearful of counterfeit *solidi*, demanded that most of the gold given them be in the form of ingots or gold bars. It was estimated that seventy-two *solidi* equaled a pound of gold. Because the Huns did not mint their own currency, they used some of the gold to barter for other goods at seasonal fairs. Gold was also used to make jewelry, crowns, and plaques.

the White Huns into the Hunnic confederation. Because the White Huns lived in central Asia, they had trading connections with the Far East. The alliance Attila made with them increased his ability to extend the Huns' trading capabilities into countries as far away as China. Attila attained their cooperation through both his skill as a negotiator and his willingness to use barbarous methods when necessary.

Attila was a brutal leader who treated harshly those who resisted his domination. Groups who fought back incurred his wrath, and their tribes and settlements were destroyed. On the other hand, the barbarian tribes who submitted and accepted the Huns as their overlords were allowed to keep their lands, their traditions, and their own laws. They were also permitted to keep their own religious beliefs and practices. As long as they paid an annual tribute in gold to the Huns and agreed to participate in their military campaigns, they were able to live in much the same way they always had.

The Huns Continue to Bait the Eastern Roman Empire

By 440 the Hunnic territories controlled by Bleda and Attila stretched from Hungary eastward to central Asia and from the Baltic Sea in the north to Persia in the south. While Attila was occupied with fighting along the outer borders of the Huns' empire, however, he had not been able to enforce the terms Theodosius had agreed upon in the Peace of Margus. During some years Theodosius failed to pay the seven hundred pounds of gold he had promised to the Huns, and he had allowed many fugitives to remain in the eastern empire because he needed their service as mercenaries in his army. Knowing that the Huns would eventually retaliate, in 439 he ordered that the high wall that had earlier been built to the west of Constantinople be fortified and extended to the sea. Theodosius believed the wall would protect his capital.

In the meantime, during 439 and 440, the power of both the eastern and western empires was being challenged on several fronts. The Persians attacked Roman Armenia in what is today eastern Turkey, threatening the security of the eastern empire. The western empire was menaced by the Vandals, a Germanic barbarian tribe who threatened an invasion of Sicily in the south of Italy. Theodosius sent military aid to the western empire to help it repel this attack.

Theodosius II had these walls, still standing today, built to protect Constantinople from attack by Attila and the Huns.

When Bleda and Attila learned of the Romans' preoccupations with these uprisings, they decided it was a good time to plunder the Balkans, a territory that includes modern-day Bulgaria. Their first move was an attack against the Roman fort of Castra Constantia on the Danube River. At a nearby marketplace all the traders were slaughtered or captured.

Although this attack violated the terms of the Peace of Margus, the Huns justified it by claiming that Romans, under orders from the bishop of Margus, had secretly come in to their territory and looted treasure buried in the graves of former Hunnic kings. They also accused the Romans of continuing to grant refuge to fugitives from the Hun territories. The Romans did not deny these accusations. In retaliation, the Huns ordered the Romans to hand over the bishop of Margus and the remaining fugitives.

When Theodosius refused, Attila and Bleda had an excuse for war. In 440 they crossed the Danube River and advanced on the towns and forts on the southern banks. They leveled the city of Viminacium, now the site of the town of Kostolacz. All the survivors of the attack were killed or taken as slaves.

A short truce followed. But the next year, 441, the Huns attacked Margus, and were easily able to take the city. The bishop, believing that the Huns could not be stopped, opened the gates of the city himself after receiving assurances of his personal safety. It is not known whether the bishop survived the attack.

The town was destroyed, and many citizens were massacred. The Huns did not encounter resistance from the Romans, who were occupied with campaigns in other parts of the empire.

The Huns Advance

The Huns had taken advantage of the Roman army's preoccupation with fighting in other parts of the Mediterranean to add to their territories. The eastern Roman army, which had been left to defend Constantinople, had suffered great defeats by the Huns, who now controlled much of the Greek frontier and the territories of present-day Albania, Bulgaria, and Yugoslavia. Historians do not know the reasons leading to a truce between the eastern Romans and the Huns in 442, but during that year there was a short period of relative peace. Up to this time it appears that Bleda had been the dominant leader of the Huns, but Attila's power was growing. He had been in correspondence with Constantinople demanding the payment of tribute and had independently attacked some imperial fortresses.

In 443 Theodosius continued to ignore Attila's demand that he return the fugitives and deliver the gold he owed to the Huns under the terms of the Peace of Margus. Angered by the emperor's refusal, Attila began to devastate the Roman territory, attacking forts along the Danube. When Attila was able to capture the Roman city of Ratiaria, he totally destroyed it and took

The Horses of the Huns

Horses played an important part in the Huns' lifestyle and economy. As the Huns settled across the steppes of central Asia, they domesticated wild horses, which they used to pull their wagons and carts during their migrations across central Asia. They rode horses as a means of transportation and for herding sheep. Horses were also a source of food, providing milk and meat. Their hides were used as material for clothing and tents.

By 1000 B.C. the Hunnic warriors from the steppes of central Asia had learned to use horses in warfare. In battles, the mounted warriors would pretend to flee. Then they would rapidly turn their horses around and shoot a volley of arrows at their unsuspecting enemy. Their adroit maneuvering on horseback gave them a great advantage over the barbarian and Roman foot soldiers, who mainly used horses to pull their wagons and chariots. Although some of the Romans also fought on horseback, they would usually dismount to fight.

The Huns' horses were of a smaller and stockier breed than those of their adversaries. Their appearance was described by the Roman veterinarian Vegetius Renatus in The World of the Huns, *by Otto J. Maenchen-Helfen:*

Hardy creatures, accustomed to cold and frost, the horses of the barbarians need neither stables nor medical care. The Roman horse is of a much more delicate constitution; unless it has good shelter and a warm stable it will catch one illness after another. . . . They have great hooked heads, protruding eyes, narrow nostrils, broad jaws, strong and stiff necks, manes hanging below the knees, overlarge ribs, curved backs, bushy tails, cannon bones of great strength . . . wide-spreading hooves, hollow loins; their bodies are angular, with no fat on the rump or muscles of the back, their stature inclining to length rather than to height, the belly drawn, the bones huge. The very thinness of these horses is pleasing, and there is beauty even in their ugliness.

its inhabitants as slaves. The victory had a strategic value to the Huns because control of this city protected them from a Roman attack from the rear. Bleda's role in this campaign is not known.

The Huns seemed unstoppable. They next attacked and destroyed the town of Naissus, or Nish, the birthplace of the emperor Constantine. This heavily populated city was also the site of the Roman arms factory. Through these campaigns the Huns were able to capture a large number of prisoners and gain a fortune in loot.

The next towns they attacked opened the way to the capital city of Constantinople. Theodosius's forces, although commanded by the most skilled generals in the eastern Roman army, were unable to hold back the Huns, who dealt them heavy defeats outside Constantinople. The Huns reached the sea at three points near the city, but they were stopped by the massive walls that had been built around it. Even so, the devastating losses suffered by the Romans finally forced Theodosius to negotiate with the Huns.

The First Peace of Anatolius

Theodosius sent Anatolius, one of his most skilled diplomats and the commander of the soldiers in the eastern empire, to negotiate with Attila. The Hun was also ready to negotiate. Attila's troops had been weakened by an outbreak of malaria and dysentery. He doubted that his army could penetrate the heavy fortifications that surrounded Constantinople. Moreover, he was satisfied with the amount of valuable plunder that he and his men had been able to capture during the campaign. The Huns were aware that their many victories and the destruction they had caused the Romans gave them an upper hand in the negotiations.

The terms Attila demanded were harsh. He ordered the Romans to immediately pay the Huns the six thousand pounds of gold they owed since signing the Peace of Margus in 435. And they were again ordered to immediately return all the fugitives and were forbidden

to receive any further escapees. After the Romans agreed to these terms, the treaty was signed on August 27, 443.

The Romans claimed that they had voluntarily agreed to the terms of the treaty, but in reality they were fearful of the power of Attila's army. The army had depleted their treasury, so to raise money for the tribute, the emperor forced everyone to pay an enormous war tax. The result on the population of Constantinople was devastating. To raise funds to pay the tax, some men were forced to sell their furniture and their wives' jewelry in the marketplace. Others, contemplating financial ruin, committed suicide.

A short time later Attila sent Scottas, one of his trusted lieutenants, to Constantinople to collect the gold and the fugitives. Theodosius agreed to hand over the gold, but he stated that the Romans had killed all the escapees who had refused to return to the Huns. Attila rejected this claim, and he continued to send his ambassadors to Constantinople to demand the return of the fugitives. He may have had a devious reason for his actions. Notes historian E.A. Thompson, "Attila merely sent the embassies so that those of his followers who served on them might reap the rich harvest of costly presents which the Roman government found it expedient to supply."[17] Thus, Attila's repeated demands enabled his ambassadors to receive valuable gifts, some of which ultimately ended up in his own treasury, creating a nonviolent victory for the Huns. His power was growing.

This relief shows Roman tax collectors counting coins. The Romans were forced to pay huge sums to Attila and the Huns to keep peace.

Bleda's Death

Attila had taken advantage of the eastern campaigns to reinforce his reputation as a fearless, effective leader. It appears that his leadership was stronger than that of Bleda. Marcel Brion writes, "[Bleda] satisfied himself with the pleasures that hunting and orgies furnished him."[18] Sometime in 445 A.D. (some scholars say 443) Bleda died. Some accounts say that he died in a hunting accident, but soon after his death, rumors began to circulate that Attila had killed him.

The death of his brother removed any challenges to Attila's claims as leader of the unified Hunnic empire. The ter-ritories and people Bleda had ruled came under Attila's control, increasing his power. During his first eleven years as coleader of the Huns, he had managed to unite the various Hunnic tribes of central Europe as a powerful military force that had openly challenged the power of the Eastern Roman Empire, winning territories and wealth both through violent confrontation and cunning negotiation. The wealth of the Huns had substantially increased, along with their growing power, and the devastation they had caused spread fear among anyone who might consider defying Attila.

Chapter Three

Attila's Conquests in the East

Bleda was buried with pomp and ceremony due to his high rank as king. In attendance at the funeral were tribal chiefs, military leaders, and royalty from the areas controlled by the Huns. Attila was now positioned to rule over all the Huns, including those who had formerly been governed by Bleda. From that time until his own death, Attila would not have any serious contender for the leadership of the Huns and their allied barbarian tribes. His actions were now motivated by his desire for more power.

A Strange Dream

Shortly after Bleda's funeral Attila had a prophetic dream in which an elderly man appeared from the sky and presented him with a sword. When a whirlwind suddenly picked Attila up, he was taken over the plains and mountains of Europe. As he slashed through the air with the sword, waters parted and cities in his path were destroyed.

When he awoke, he asked his shamans to interpret the dream for him. They told him that soon he would find the sacred sword of the Huns, which would enable him to conquer the world. According to Hunnic legends, the sword was a sacred weapon that the Huns had won years before from the Scythians, a related barbarian tribe who lived in modern-day Russia. Years before Attila's birth the sword had been lost. For the Huns, as well as for many barbarian tribes, the sword probably represented the god of war. Attila believed that this dream was an omen that would ensure his future successes.

Not long after Attila had the dream, a shepherd came to his court with a strange

This painting depicts Attila's dream of receiving the sword of the Huns, which symbolized the god of war. Attila believed this destined him to rule the world.

story. This visit was later described by the Greco-Roman historian Priscus:

> When a certain shepherd beheld one heifer of his flock limping and could find no cause of this wound, he anxiously followed the trail of blood and at length came to a sword it had unwittingly trampled while nibbling the grass. He dug it up and took it straight to Attila. The king rejoiced at this gift, and being ambitious, thought he had been appointed ruler of the whole world, and that through the sword . . . supremacy in all wars was assured to him.[19]

The discovery of a sword, whether or not it was the sacred sword of the Huns, gave Attila great motivation to rule over both the Eastern and Western Roman empires and inspired him with a belief in

The Barbarian Tribes

In the third and fourth centuries, as the Roman Empire was disintegrating, tribes from the north began to invade territories belonging to the empire. The Romans called these people *barbarians*, a term that referred to those who lived outside the boundaries of the empire and who could not speak and read Greek and Latin, which were considered the languages of culture and education. Some linguists believe that the word came from the harsh sounds of their languages that to Roman and Greek ears sounded like "bar-bar." Others believe that the word comes from Greek and meant stranger or outsider.

The migrations of barbarian tribes had begun during the last centuries B.C. and continued for the first four centuries A.D. During this period the barbarian populations of northern and central Europe increased, creating a need for new land on which to expand.

There were many different barbarian tribes. The Goths were a Germanic group that was divided into two major tribes: the Ostrogoths, who in the fifth century occupied much of Italy, and the Visigoths, who lived in Gaul (France) and Spain. The Alani were nomads from southeastern Russia who moved westward when they were attacked by the Huns. Some Alani ultimately joined the Huns; others joined the Vandals, another Germanic people who invaded modern-day France in 406. Yet another Germanic people, the Franks, also occupied part of northern France and Belgium.

Barbarians sometimes fought against Attila, and sometimes they were allied with him. Likewise, they sometimes fought for the Romans and at other times attacked them. The threat from various barbarian tribes eventually resulted in the collapse of the Western Roman Empire in 476, when it fell to Germanic invaders.

his ability to win. Anyone who challenged his right to do this, including those who had formerly paid allegiance to Bleda, would have to fight both the king and his supposedly divine powers.

Constantinople Is Vulnerable

Despite Attila's confidence that he would eventually make great conquests, the first years of his reign were relatively peaceful. Soon, however, conditions in the eastern empire made the Romans in Constantinople a vulnerable target. Until 447, their relationship with the Huns was less important to the eastern Romans than the conflicts that created instability on their other borders. In the east the Persian Empire was a continuing threat, and the Vandals made periodic raids by land and by sea. During this period the Eastern Roman Empire also suffered from many disasters, both natural and man-made. The winter of 443–444 was particularly severe, causing thousands to die from the cold. In 444 heavy rainstorms destroyed towns and estates in Bithynia in the northwestern part of the empire. In 445 riots in Constantinople resulted in many deaths. The people also suffered from a lack of food and several epidemics of the deadly plague.

Political intrigues in Theodosius's court contributed to the instability. The emperor had recently appointed a shrewd adviser, Chrysaphius Zstommas, as chief administrator of Constantinople. Chrysaphius was a corrupt man who secretly robbed from the government and was hated by almost everyone. The power-hungry Chrysaphius relished his new powers. C.D. Gordon writes that he "controlled everything, plundering the possessions of all and being hated by all."[20] His actions added to the atmosphere of tension that spread through the city in 446 and 447.

Attila Builds His Army

As Constantinople weakened, Attila grew more powerful. By 447 he was at the height of his leadership abilities. Sensing the vulnerability of Constantinople, he decided that his army would strike at the eastern empire when milder weather arrived in the spring, the traditional time for beginning military campaigns. Acquiring more territory was not his only motivation for initiating an aggressive action. His economy depended largely on the plunder the Huns would grab from the areas they attacked and the tribute money they extorted from the Romans.

The Huns' army included soldiers from barbarian tribes, such as the Goths and the Gepids, that Attila had conquered earlier. Many of the soldiers, armed with bows and arrows, lances, and spears, were mounted on stocky, fast-moving horses. Others were foot soldiers. They were a formidable force.

The army of the Huns had gained a fearsome reputation for violence and cruelty. The Roman historian Ammianus Marcellinus described the Hun

The Huns' ferocity in battle became legendary. A thousand years later, this Renaissance painting showed Hun archers attacking a Roman city.

forces as being lightly equipped so that they could easily break into smaller groups who launched brutal attacks while frightening their adversaries with horrific screams and shouts. He added:

> You would not hesitate to call them the most terrible of all warriors, because they fight from a distance with missiles having a sharp bone, instead of their usual points, joined to the shafts with wonderful skill; then they gallop over the intervening spaces and fight hand to hand with swords regardless of their own lives; and while the enemy are guarding against wounds from sword-thrusts, they throw strips of cloth plaited into nooses over their opponents and so entangle them that they fetter their limbs and take from them the power of riding or walking.[21]

In earlier combats the Huns had relied on their traditional methods of warfare, which involved lightning attacks by mounted horsemen. As their territories expanded, however, they discovered that a cavalry was not sufficient to capture fortresses and walled cities, so their tactics

The Huns' Weapons

The weapons used by the Huns helped them achieve victory. One of their most important was the bow. The Huns were excellent archers who could shoot at targets while riding their horses at full speed. The arrows they shot were made of bone and had sharp points. Composite bows, which have a laminated construction using more than one material such as wood, sinew, or horn, have been found in the tombs of Hunnic warriors. These were probably made by craftsmen in workshops.

Swords and long lances were also used by both the Huns and the Romans. Some lances were nearly ten feet long. The pointed lance head could be up to a foot long. The Huns also threw lassos, made of strips of cloth braided into a noose, over their opponents to immobilize them.

To protect themselves from wounds, the warriors wore body armor over their torsos. Some of the warriors who came from prominent families owned metal armor, which was passed down from one generation to the next. Other warriors may have worn breastplates made of bone or horn that were stitched together with the sinews of horses or oxen. Armor was also made of chain mail, woven metal wires that created flexible protection. The thorax was a piece of armor made of metal that protected the torso on all sides. To protect their head, warriors wore helmets.

changed. To capture fortified cities, Attila's army used heavy wooden beams mounted on wheels, which they pushed close to the city walls. Armed soldiers standing on the beams were able to shoot arrows at fighters who stood on the battlements above defending their town. The invaders were protected by screens made of willow twigs woven together with rawhide and leather. Another weapon was the battering ram, a beam with a metal head that the Huns forced toward the walls, crushing them. Afterward the Huns set up scaling ladders to allow them to climb over the crumbled walls. The combination of mounted warriors, foot soldiers, and machines of war made Attila's army an almost unstoppable force.

Constantinople Prepares for an Attack

While the Huns gathered their forces, several natural disasters struck Constantinople. In January a series of earthquakes destroyed many buildings and leveled fifty-seven towers in the protective walls that surrounded the city. They also created holes in the walls. A few days after the earthquakes, a heavy rainfall caused even more damage. Buildings collapsed, and many inhabitants were buried under the ruins. The earthquakes and rain were followed by an outbreak of the plague that killed thousands. The disasters not only caused many deaths but further weakened the defenses of the eastern empire.

Fearing an attack by the Huns, the citizens of Constantinople quickly moved to rebuild and improve the fortifications in the defensive wall. A second wall was built in front of the original one to provide more protection. Within sixty days, just as Attila's armies were approaching, the repairs were completed, forming a barrier 190 to 207 feet thick and over 100 feet high. The cost of repairing the walls had drained the empire's treasury, however, and Theodosius could not pay the annual tribute to the Huns. This gave Attila a good excuse to attack.

Attila Attacks

The first major conflicts between the Huns and the Romans took place in an area called Dacia in what is now southeastern Europe between the lower Danube River and the Carpathian Mountains. Rather than allowing Attila to come close enough to Constantinople to attack, the Roman commander Arnegliscus engaged the Huns at a site a distance away from the city. The battle was ferocious. The Romans had a strong defense, but in the end they were defeated by Attila's forces. The battle had been the fiercest confrontation that Attila had encountered up to this time.

Attila used his military skills to determine his next course of action. Aware that his army might not be able to scale the massive walls around Constantinople, he turned his troops away from the city and diverted them deeper into Thrace, a region in the eastern Balkan

An engraving depicts Constantinople during the time of Attila. While Attila's forces destroyed the surrounding regions, the city's walls kept him at bay.

peninsula that encompasses present-day Greece, Albania, and parts of Turkey. The Huns destroyed everything in their path and advanced to Marcianople, a large city the Romans used as a base, where they captured and razed the town. They then overran much of Greece, causing destruction wherever they went. Callinicus, a Roman Christian who was a witness to much of the devastation, wrote that more than a hundred towns were captured and there were more dead than could be counted.

Attila and his army were accused of many atrocities. In addition to leveling many towns and killing the residents or taking them as slaves, they destroyed Christian monasteries and churches and killed many monks and nuns. Attila, a pagan, feared the influence the Christian clergy might have on the people under his control. The enemies of the

The Hagia Sophia church lay within the walls of Constantinople during Attila's day. Today it is a mosque.

Constantinople

The court of Theodosius II was located in Constantinople, the most important city in the Eastern Roman Empire. Constantinople, today called Istanbul, is located at the entrance to the Black Sea on the Bosporus, a 19-mile (30.58 km.) long strait that separates Europe and Asia. The city was founded by the Roman emperor Constantine after he gained control over the eastern empire and moved the capital of the Roman Empire there from Rome. The city was built on the ancient town of Byzantium, which dated back to the eighth century B.C. when it was a Greek colony. During the fourth and fifth centuries, the population of Constantinople steadily grew, and the senate located there was comparable to that of Rome.

After the fall of Rome in the late fifth century, Constantinople remained the capital of the Byzantine Empire and the center of the Eastern Orthodox Church. Portions of the walls built around the city to repel the Huns still remain, and many of the city's landmarks lie within this area. These include the famous Byzantine church known as the Hagia Sophia, the Mosque of Suleyman, and the Blue Mosque. The University of Istanbul, Turkey's oldest university, was founded in 1453.

Huns also accused them of eating the flesh of children and drinking the blood of women, but these claims have not been proven. Nevertheless, the Huns did cause much destruction. A Roman named Count Marcellinus later wrote, "Attila ground almost the whole of Europe into dust."[22]

The Second Peace of Anatolius

After his success in the Balkans, Attila pondered his next move. The Romans in Constantinople fearfully waited for him to attack, but he had another plan in mind. In a shrewd move, Attila decided not to attack Constantinople after all. His reasons were twofold: He probably feared that his army could not break through the newly reinforced walls protecting the city, and his forces were once again weakened by malaria and dysentery. Thousands of his soldiers died from the illnesses, and those who survived were too weak to fight. Writer Isaac of Antioch later wrote:

God conquered the tyrant. . . . Through sickness he laid low the Huns. . . . The sinners drew the bow and put their arrows on the string . . . and the host [Huns] were on the point of coming quickly—then sickness blew through it [Huns] and hurled the host into wilderness. He

Attila and his Huns caused so much destruction that it seemed that "Attila and his Huns ground almost the whole of Europe into dust."

whose heart was strong for battle waxed feeble through sickness. He who was skilled in shooting with the bow, sickness of the bowels overthrew him—the riders of the steed slumbered and slept and the cruel army silenced.[23]

The illness among his troops stopped Attila for a time, but his earlier victories still caused terror among the Romans. Believing that the Huns would eventually attack Constantinople, Theodosius was forced to beg for a truce, and he sent Anatolius to meet with Attila. Considering the Huns' victories, Anatolius was not in a good position to win concessions.

Attila's demands for peace were harsh. He ordered the Romans to immediately pay the back tribute of six thousand pounds of gold, and he also demanded a new annual payment of twenty-one hundred pounds of gold. His next demand was especially dangerous for the eastern Romans. He ordered that a large territory south of the Danube be cleared of all people, both Roman and peasants. The area had already been devastated by his army, and the land was covered with the bones of men killed in the war. The loss of the land would push the Romans away from the Danube River and remove a buffer zone between their territory and that of the Huns.

To maintain a peaceful relationship with the Huns, Theodosius had no recourse but to agree to this extreme demand. As time went by, the peasants slowly began to come back to their fields, but the Romans were not allowed to return. Maenchen-Helfen writes, "The Huns aimed at one thing: at pushing the Romans back from the Danube, thereby removing the main obstacle that could prevent them [Huns] from breaking into the empire."[24]

To pay for the cost of the war and to meet Attila's new demands for gold, the Romans had to raise taxes. Again, some wealthy citizens had to sell their valuables

Attila, depicted here as a king, wielded a great deal of power after he conquered much of Europe.

Attila's Advisers

Attila surrounded himself with advisers from different cultures who reflected a variety of opinions. While most of these men were fluent in the Hunnic language, they could also communicate in Latin, Greek, and the various languages of the barbarians. Onegesius, Attila's most powerful adviser and closest friend, served as court chamberlain or prime minister. His brother, Scottas, was responsible for collecting tribute. After the first treaty of Anatolius, Attila had entrusted him with obtaining the gold and fugitives from the Romans. The origins of the two brothers are not known, but they were influenced by Greek culture.

Constantius, Attila's principal secretary, was born in Italy and was fluent in Latin. He may have been sent to Attila by Aëtius as a token of friendship. Orestes, another Roman, came to Attila's court from the Roman province of Noricum. He assumed an important position and along with Edeco, who was known for his military skill, was sent to Constantinople to negotiate with Chrysaphius and Theodosius.

These men and other important advisers helped maintain Attila's authority. They served as ambassadors to the outside world, where they negotiated treaties and collected the rich gifts that all ambassadors received. At home in Pannonia, they guarded Attila and gave him advice based on their diverse experience and backgrounds. They were also assigned their own military force, enabling them to rule over different regions of the Huns' empire. During battles they commanded the subject soldiers from the areas they controlled.

to pay the new taxes. Attila had also continued to demand that anyone who had changed loyalty from the Huns to the Romans be returned to him. When the Romans told these recruits that they had to return or face execution, some of them chose death rather than going back to face punishment from the Huns.

The war of 447 was a triumph for Attila in many ways. After Bleda's death he had assumed the position of authority, but it had taken his victories to firmly establish his power. Through the campaigns he had gained greater wealth and control over vast territories. His authority was now unquestioned. As Maenchen-Helfen notes, "The victory was *his* victory. From 447, Attila, king, commander in chief, supreme judge, was unconditionally obeyed."[25]

Chapter Four

A Plot to Kill Attila

The years following Attila's invasion of the Eastern Roman Empire were relatively peaceful. The battles and negotiations of 447 had left the Romans at a severe disadvantage in their dealings with the Huns. Financially strapped by Attila's demands for more gold and weakened by the devastation in much of the eastern empire, the Romans now had to rely on their skills at negotiation to maintain a degree of stability with the Huns. The Romans, however, knew that Attila was still a threat, and the chief administrator, Chrysaphius, sought a way to do away with him. In the meantime, Attila focused his attention on barbarian tribes living along the borders of the territories he controlled.

In 448 Attila became concerned about a relatively obscure barbarian tribe called the Acatziri who lived in an area near the Black Sea in what is today Russia. Little is known about these people, but it is believed that they may have been an independent tribe of Huns that was not associated with Attila's growing confederation of allied tribes. The Acatziri came to the attention of eastern Romans, who wanted an ally living in a strategic location at the eastern edge of Attila's territory. To create this alliance Theodosius sent gifts to the Acatziri chieftains. When Attila learned about the Romans' tactics, he sent a military force to conquer the Acatziri. After defeating them, he installed his eldest son, Ellak, as a ruler over them. Soon, another event caused him to become even more irritated with the eastern empire.

Attila Is Angry

The economy of Attila's kingdom was based on receiving tribute from the

A painting shows the Hunnic army disembarking from their boats. That Attila named his son "Sea-Storm" may hint that the Huns did use boats.

Romans, so when in 449 the eastern empire again began to renege on its agreement to send gold, Attila became angry. The government in Constantinople was beset by financial problems and wanted to get out of the agreement. The hated tax collectors had demanded money and precious objects from everyone to provide the payment owed to the Huns, but much of what they collected ended up in the pockets of corrupt officials, leaving insufficient funds in the empire's treasury. When Attila's ambassadors demanded immediate payment of the tribute money, Theodosius's response was to argue for a reduction in the amount owed.

Early in 449 Attila sent a delegation to Constantinople for further negotiations. The delegation was led by Edeco and Orestes, two of Attila's most powerful and skilled ambassadors. The two men were rivals who distrusted each other. Edeco, a barbarian, was a military man who commanded many of Attila's regiments. Orestes, a Roman by birth, had gained Attila's trust with his diplomatic skills. Attila used the two men's dislike of each other to his advantage because he believed that they would not band together to betray him. He instructed them to deliver a letter to the Romans ordering them to send a delegation of their highest ambassadors to meet with him to discuss the disagreements between the two powers. Attila, who was not above using blackmail to get his way, worded the demand to imply that a refusal would result in a renewal of hostilities.

The Delegates Arrive in Constantinopole

When the two ambassadors arrived in Constantinople, they handed over letters from Attila to Chrysaphius, who by now had acquired almost complete control over the government in Constantinople. Attila again demanded full and immediate payment of the tri-bute money and the return of any Huns who remained under Roman protection, threatening to attack if these demands were not met.

Because few Romans could speak the language of the Huns, communications between them and Attila's representatives were made through Bigilas, a Roman interpreter who spoke both the Hunnic language and Latin. In spite of the undercurrent of hostility, the Romans received the two Huns with pomp and ceremony and gave them a tour of the lavish imperial palace.

The Romans Tempt Edeco

The two Hun ambassadors were greatly impressed by the elegance of Theodosius's palace, one of the most luxurious buildings in the world at that time. When Edeco expressed his amazement at its splendor, Chrysaphius took him aside and, through Bigilas, told him that

The Language of the Huns

Little is known about the language spoken by the Huns. The difficulty of studying it is complicated by the fact that the language they spoke was not written down. Seventh-century writers say that the Huns' language was similar to that of the Bulgars, a Turkish tribe that lived near the southern Balkans.

One way scholars have tried to reconstruct the Huns' language is through the few words of the language that are known. Some of these are the same in both Hunnish and Turkish. For example, "girl" is kiz, and "god" is tengri in both languages. The names of some prominent Huns also have meaning in Turkish. Dengizik, son of Attila, means sea storm. Csaba, another son, means shepherd.

a gold-roofed house could be his if he took up Roman ways. He then questioned Edeco about his relationship with Attila, asking if he ever met with the Hun leader alone. Edeco responded that he was both a close friend of Attila and one of those entrusted with guarding him. Chrysaphius said he would like to make him an offer that would be personally advantageous to him, but that discretion was required. He then invited Edeco to join him for a private dinner at his residence later that day.

That night, at a feast in Chrysaphius's house, the two men spoke through Bigilas and swore themselves to secrecy. Chrysaphius promised Edeco great wealth and titles from the Romans in Constantinople if he would assassinate Attila. The Hun expressed interest and asked Chrysaphius to give him fifty pounds of gold to bribe people he would need to help him with the murder.

After Edeco left, Chrysaphius hurried to tell Theodosius about the assassination plot. The emperor agreed to the scheme, and plans were made for a delegation of Romans to accompany the Huns back to Attila's encampment in accordance with Attila's demands. Theodosius assigned a high-ranking, skilled Roman diplomat named Maximinus, who did not know about the assassination plot, as leader of the delegation. His job was to act as ambassador and to speak to Attila face to face to respond to the threats contained in the letters. Maximinus persuaded Priscus, a Greco-Roman

historian who also served as his friend and adviser, to accompany the delegation. Priscus's written account of the journey provides one of the few eyewitness descriptions of life in Attila's court and country.

The Journey to Attila's Court

The delegation, made up of Romans and Huns including Orestes and Edeco, left Constantinople on horseback in the early summer of 449. Seventeen fugitive Huns whose return had been demanded by Attila also accompanied the group. The journey to the court of Attila took many weeks. Along the way the Romans viewed firsthand the devastation caused by Attila's army. Historian E.A. Thompson writes, "Six years had passed since the Huns had captured Naissus, but no effort had yet been made to bring back life to the ruins. The ambassador and his party did not even try to pitch their tents inside the wall, and, since the river bank immediately outside it was covered with the bones of those who had been slain in the fighting, they went upstream a short distance until they found a clear space where they might encamp."[26] The destruction Attila had caused made the Romans apprehensive about what would happen in their upcoming negotiations with him.

When the delegation finally arrived at Attila's encampment, the Romans and the Huns separated, and the Huns continued on to Attila's court. It is believed that Edeco told Attila about the

Ancient Roman historians, who viewed the Huns with disgust, probably influenced history's negative view of Attila.

assassination plot almost immediately, but Attila kept the information to himself. Rather than taking quick action against the Romans, Attila decided that he would try to keep them off balance to maintain control over them during the negotiations. At times he would be rude, and at other times, polite.

Later that afternoon, a group of Huns confronted the Romans and told them they could not pitch their tents on a nearby hillside because Attila's encampment was in the valley below and it would be disrespectful for their camp to be in a higher position than his. The Romans, concerned for their own safety and not wanting to irritate their hosts, then made their camp in a location chosen by the Huns. Later, a delegation of high-ranking Huns led by Scottas, Edeco, and Orestes arrived and rudely demanded to know why the Romans had come to

Pannonia. This confused the Romans since Attila had demanded that a delegation come to negotiate with him. When Maximinus responded that the emperor had ordered them to deal directly with Attila in person, the Huns brusquely ordered the Romans to leave. The behavior of the Huns stunned and perplexed the Romans.

Maximinus, fearing an outbreak of hostilities, decided that it would probably be wise to obey and ordered his ser-

Priscus at the Court of Attila

Much of what is known about Attila's court comes from the writings of the Greco-Roman historian Priscus, who traveled from Constantinople with the Roman delegation led by Maximinus to negotiate with Attila. His writings, which reveal the Roman bias against barbarian cultures, are the basis for much of the negative reputation attributed to Attila. In the following excerpt from his work Fragmenta Historicum Graecorum, *translated by J.B. Bury, Priscus describes an incident that occurred in the house of Attila's lieutenant Onegesius.*

When I arrived at the house, along with the attendants who carried the gifts, I found the doors closed, and had to wait until some one should come out and announce our arrival. As I waited and walked up and down in front of the enclosure which surrounded the house, a man, whom from his Scythian [Hunnic] dress I took for a barbarian, came up and addressed me in Greek, with the word *Xaire,* "Hail!" I was surprised at a Scythian speaking Greek. For the subjects of the Huns, swept together from various lands, speak besides their own barbarous tongues, either Hunnic or Gothic, or—as many have commercial dealings with the western Romans—Latin; but none of them easily speak Greek. …This man resembled a well-to-do Scythian, being well dressed, and having his hair cut in a circle after Scythian fashion. Having returned his salutation, I asked him who he was and whence he had come into a foreign land and adopted Scythian life. … Then he smiled and said that he had been born a Greek and had gone as a merchant to Viminacium, on the Danube, where he stayed a long time, and married a very rich wife. But the city fell prey to the barbarians, and he was stript of his prosperity, and on account of his riches was allotted to Onegesius in the division of the spoil, as it was the custom among the Scythians for the chiefs to reserve for themselves the rich prisoners. Having fought bravely against the Romans and the Acatiri, he had paid the spoils he won to his master, and so obtained freedom. He then married a barbarian wife and had children, and had the privilege of eating at the table of Onegesius.

vants to prepare for the delegation's return to Roman territory. Bigilas, the only person in the delegation who knew of the assassination plot and who wanted it to proceed as planned, scolded the Romans, saying that their delegation would be a failure if they left without meeting Attila. The Romans, however, continued their preparations to leave. Seeing that Maximinus was upset by the apparent failure of his delegation, his friend Priscus took Scottas aside and told him that if he could convince Attila to meet with the Romans he and his leader would receive the rich gifts they had brought. The mention of valuable gifts convinced Attila to finally meet with the Romans, and a short time later they were summoned to his tent.

The Romans Meet Attila

When the Romans entered Attila's tent, they found him seated on a simple wooden chair rather than a throne. Priscus described the Hun's appearance in his account of the trip. According to Thompson, "He [Priscus] observed the short, squat body and the huge face, with its small, deep-set eyes, and found little to admire in the flat nose and the few straggling hairs which took the place of a beard."[27]

Attila treated the Romans rudely, but his anger was particularly severe against Bigilas, whom he called a shameless beast that he would kill if he were not protected by his high-ranking position as translator for the Romans. Bigi-

las was stunned and confused by this outburst. The Hun then angrily insisted that there were still many fugitive Huns living under Roman protection and demanded their immediate return. After his secretaries read aloud the names of these individuals, Attila ordered Bigilas to return to Constantinople to negotiate a final return of the fugitives, declaring that he would not allow them to enroll in the Roman army to fight against him. Attila then ordered the Roman delegation to remain under his control until Bigilas returned from Constantinople with a solution to the hostage problem. They were told that they could not buy anything while in Hunnic territory except for food. The following day Bigilas set out for Constantinople, and the Huns, accompanied at a distance by the rest of the Roman delegation, traveled north to their home base on the Tisza River in Hungary.

The Huns Reach Attila's Village

The journey to Attila's capital took over a week. Along the way Attila stopped at a village, where he took another wife, the daughter of a tribal chief named Eskam. The delegation finally reached Attila's principal village, a town located on a treeless plain. Priscus described Attila's welcoming arrival at his home: "Maidens came to meet Attila as he entered this village, advancing before him in rows under fine white linen cloth . . . which were held up by the hands of women . . . . They sang [Hun] songs."[28] At one of the larger houses, the wife of Attila's principal adviser, Onegesius, approached and offered him a silver goblet of wine and other delicacies, which he accepted. He then proceeded to his own home, a cluster of wooden houses surrounded by a wall.

Attila Hosts a Banquet

While the Romans were staying in Attila's community, they were allowed to move about freely. On one occasion, they were invited to a banquet in Attila's palace. Priscus observed the hierarchy of power that was reflected in the seating arrangement. In the middle of the room, Attila reclined on a couch. Onegesius, as his most important lieutenant, was seated in the honorary position to his right. The Romans were seated on the left. A servant brought Attila a goblet of wine, and he toasted the Romans and other guests. Priscus also noted the simplicity of Attila's lifestyle: "While sumptuous food, served on silver plates had been prepared for the other barbarians and for us, for Attila there was nothing but meat on a wooden platter. He showed himself temperate in all other ways too, for gold and silver goblets were offered to the men at the feast, but his mug was of wood."[29]

Priscus was surprised by Attila's clothing as well, which was different from that of the other Huns present. He wrote, "His dress was plain, having care for nothing other than to be clean, nor

Roman historians described Atilla's dress as plain but an engraving shows the Hunnic ruler richly attired in flowing robes and an ornate head covering.

was the sword by his side, nor the clasps of his barbarian boots, nor the bridle of his horse, like those of the [Huns], adorned with gold or gems or anything of high price."[30]

Priscus noticed that Attila's facial expression was sullen and stern. However, his look softened when his gaze fell upon his youngest son, Ernak. One of the barbarians explained that seers had predicted that Ernak would be a future leader of the Huns.

During their stay in Attila's community, Priscus and Maximinus made many observations. They were invited to the home of Attila's principal wife, Kreka, where they were graciously received, and they also visited the home of Onegesius, where they observed his Roman-style bath and conversed with its builder, a Greek architect who had been enslaved by the Huns. They then asked for permission to return to Constantinople. Attila had obtained what he wanted—gifts—from this particular delegation. By forcing them to remain under his control, he had demonstrated that he had the upper hand. Also, his main complaint was against Bigilas and his boss, Chrysaphius. So Attila gave them permission to leave. A few days later they were given gifts and set out for the long trip home. On their journey back home, they crossed paths with Bigilas, who was returning to Attila's village with the fifty pounds of gold to pay for the murder of Attila. He was so sure of the success of the plot that he had

The Metalwork of the Huns

Although Attila favored simple attire, other Huns enjoyed ornaments made of precious materials. Archaeological sites in central Europe have revealed ornaments of gold and silver that are believed to have belonged to the Huns. Among these are gold crowns or diadems, some of which are decorated with garnets, mother-of-pearl, amber, or glass fragments. Some of the crowns are made of bronze and covered with gold sheet. Jewelry such as earrings made of gold and silver have also been found in graves.

The Huns also used copper and bronze to make cauldrons or cooking pots. These were probably made by a process known as casting in which the molten metal is poured into a mold. Large objects were cast in several pieces that were later joined. Those made by the Huns were usually of moderate size and round with handles. Archaeologists are unsure of the use of these pots. Some were probably used to boil meat, which was lifted out of the pot by a hook. Others may have had some religious significance.

brought his young son along. Bigilas was unaware that a trap awaited him.

Bigilas Is Arrested

When Bigilas arrived at Attila's village, he was immediately arrested and the gold was confiscated. He tried to explain that the money was for his food and supplies and included ransom money sent from the relatives of Romans who had been captured by the Huns. Attila revealed his knowledge of the assassination plot, roaring, "No longer, you worthless beast, will you escape justice by deception. Nor will there be any excuse sufficient for you to avoid punishment."[31]

When Attila threatened to kill Bigilas's son, the interpreter broke down in tears and confessed that he was carrying out the assassination plot planned by Chrysaphius. Rather than kill Bigilas, Attila ordered the interpreter's son to return to Constantinople to obtain an additional fifty pounds of gold as ransom for his father's life. After the son brought the gold back, Attila freed Bigilas, but forced him to wear a bag containing some of the gold around his neck. Bigilas was ordered to take this to the emperor to remind him of his part in the murder plot. Attila also demanded the execution of Chrysaphius.

During his dealings with the powerful Romans from Constantinople, Attila had kept the upper hand by keeping them off balance, shunning them at times and entertaining them at others. During their stay in his village, they had been well treated, but their destiny and safety had been in his hands. He had shown a degree of leniency toward Bigilas by not executing him, but his mercy was calculated as a way to humiliate Theodosius and the eastern empire.

In the following months Attila's position toward the eastern empire softened somewhat. He agreed to release Roman prisoners under his control without ransom, and he abandoned his demands for the death of Chrysaphius. Patrick Howarth writes, "The explanation of Attila's change of policy was, no doubt, that he was already directing his attention to other lands, and for this purpose he wanted stability and peace in his relations with the Eastern Empire."[32]

In 450 the leadership of the eastern empire changed when Theodosius died after a horseback riding accident. The power transferred to his older sister, Pulcheria, a shrewd woman who knew that the Romans would probably not accept a female ruler. To solve this dilemma, she married Marcian, a sixty-year-old general who assumed control of the government. One of Marcian's first acts was to stop the annual payment of gold to the Huns. Attila did not initially respond to this insult because his attention was now turning toward the western empire.

Chapter Five

Attila Turns His Attention West

The year 450 was filled with events that influenced Attila's next decisions. At first he was tempted to respond aggressively to Marcian's refusal to pay the tribute of twenty-one hundred pounds of gold that the Romans had agreed upon after the war of 447, but changing conditions in the Western Roman Empire also gave him a motivation to take aggressive actions against the west.

The Western Roman Empire in 450

In 450 the Western Roman Empire was administered by Attila's old friend Aëtius. Because of his military valor as a general, he had risen to the rank of patrician and served as master of the cavalry and infantry. Aëtius was a skilled diplomat and leader who was known for his

courage and integrity. The sixth-century historian St. Gregory of Tours described him: "He was of middle height, of manly condition, well shaped so that his body was neither too weak nor too weighty, active in limb, a most dexterous horseman, skilled in shooting the arrow, and strong in using the spear."[33] Although Valentinian was emperor, Aëtius was the power behind the throne.

Because Valentinian had been named emperor at the age of six, his mother, Galla Placidia, had served as regent or guardian until he reached adulthood. After he came of age, she continued as a powerful influence until her death in 450. Her death and Valentinian's weakness as a leader gave Attila an excuse to invade territories belonging to the western empire. Another reason came in the form of a message he received from

An engraving shows Aëtius presiding over the public games in Rome. Aëtius was both the power behind the Roman throne and a friend of Attila.

Honoria, the emperor's thirty-two-year-old sister.

A Strange Marriage Proposal

Although she lived in luxury in Ravenna, Honoria was dominated by her brother. As a young girl she had followed a religious life requiring vows of chastity; however, as she reached maturity she began an affair with Eugenius, the steward of her household. Honoria was an ambitious woman. When she tried to have Eugenius declared emperor, her infuriated brother responded by executing her lover and ordering her to marry a rich and trusted senator named Herculanus.

When Honoria staunchly refused to marry a man not of her own choosing, her angry brother sent her to live in Constantinople, where she came under the authority of the stern and autocratic empress, Pulcheria. To escape from this fate, she asked a messenger to secretly go to Attila for help, sending him a ring to prove the authenticity of the request. Attila interpreted this as a proposal of marriage. Viewing a marriage with Honoria as an opportunity to gain control over a large territory without going to war, he demanded half of the Western Roman Empire as a dowry.

Valentinian defiantly refused Attila's demand, saying that according to Roman law a woman, no matter how royal, was not entitled to half the empire. And he added that his sister was already promised to another man. The emperor's confidence was based on his belief that Aëtius's military skills would protect his empire from attack, but he was unaware of the huge army that Attila could assemble. Attila was torn between the need to move against the eastern empire because of Marcian's refusal to pay the annual tribute and his desire to punish Valentinian and the western Romans for refusing his

Marcian, Ruler of the Eastern Empire in 450

After the death of Theodosius II, the leadership of the Eastern Roman Empire passed to his unmarried sister Pulcheria. Knowing that her subjects were not likely to accept a woman as ruler, she married an older, distinguished general named Marcian in order to preserve the family's dynastic position. After the marriage, Marcian assumed the position of emperor of the eastern empire. A more forceful man than Theodosius, Marcian refused to submit to the demands of Attila. The eighteenth–century historian Edward Gibbon wrote of Marcian's leadership abilities in his classic book The Decline and Fall of the Roman Empire.

The behavior of Marcian in private life, and afterwards on the throne, may support a more rational belief that he was qualified to restore and invigorate an empire which had been almost dissolved by the successive weakness of two hereditary monarchs. He was born in Thrace, and educated to the profession of arms; but Marcian's youth had been severely exercised by poverty and misfortune, since his only resource, when he first arrived at Constantinople, consisted in two hundred pieces of gold, which he had borrowed of a friend. He passed nineteen years in the domestic and military service of Aspar and his son Ardaburius; followed those powerful generals to the Persian and African wars; and obtained by their influence, the honorable rank of tribune and senator. His mild disposition and useful talents, without alarming the jealousy, recommended Marcian to the esteem and favor of his patrons.

As emperor, Marcian refused to submit to Attila's demands.

demand for half the empire as Honoria's dowry. He sent delegations to Ravenna and Constantinople to further state his claims, but their arguments were rejected by both courts. As Attila pondered his next move, another incident helped him finally reach a decision.

Toward the end of 450 Attila received news that the king of the Ripuarian Frankish Confederation, a barbarian group living along the Rhine River, had died, creating an unstable situation in the area. Both of the king's sons claimed the throne. The elder appealed to Attila for help, while the younger asked for assistance from Aëtius and the western empire. Attila's support of the older son in order to have an ally in this strategic location gave him another reason to move against the western Romans. Rather than attacking them in Italy, their homeland, he decided to move his army west toward the Roman territory known as Gaul.

Attila Moves Toward Gaul

Early in 451 Attila began to assemble his forces in preparation for his attack on Gaul. Moving west out of Pannonia, his army gathered men from the different tribes that owed allegiance to him. Although the exact route is unknown, it is likely that the army, made up of Gepids, Ostrogoths, Skirians, Swabians, and Alemans as well as Huns, followed Roman roads toward the Danube River, passing through what is modern Hungary and Austria. When they reached the Rhine River, in what is today Ger-

many, they were joined by a powerful ally, the Franks. By this time Attila's army reportedly numbered between 250,000 and half a million men. Approximately 100,000 were mounted warriors. The rest of the army was made up of foot soldiers. The huge force created a feeling of terror and panic in the towns through which they passed.

Commanding such a diverse army presented difficulties for Attila and his lieutenants. Communication was a problem because the multiethnic force spoke many languages. Also, because many of the men were unfamiliar with the Huns' methods of fighting, it was necessary to train them in the techniques of warfare. Keeping such a large force under control fell to Onegesius and Attila's son Ellak, who trained the multinational troops to fight as one. Supplying provisions for such a massive force also took planning. In addition to the large number of siege machines and armaments needed, enormous amounts of food for the men and fodder for their horses were required to keep the army going.

As the huge mass of men approached Roman territories, Attila divided it into three separate groups to make it more manageable. He kept the largest group under his own command. In late February or early March the Huns and their allies crossed the Rhine River into what is now Luxembourg and moved through the Moselle Valley, capturing Trier, a city that was also known as Roma Segunda. They then moved

The Romans and Huns engage in a bloody battle in Gaul. It was in Gaul that Attila was dubbed the "Scourge of God."

into Gaul, causing panic throughout the countryside.

Attila Is Called the "Scourge of God"

Attila believed that brutally destroying the towns in the beginning stages of a campaign would make it easier to conquer the rest of the cities in Gaul. One of the first towns to suffer devastation was Metz, a religious and military center. On April 7, 451, the Huns placed a siege around the town to soften its resistance. Then they overran the city, burning

61

Geneviève Saves Paris

As Attila and his army approached Paris, at that time a small fortified town on an island in the Seine River, the inhabitants panicked in the knowledge that many cities had already been destroyed by the Huns. Many residents had gone to church to pray for protection. Among them was a teenage nun named Geneviève who from the age of seven had dedicated herself to a life of faith and good deeds. Standing before the congregation of frightened Parisians, Geneviève offered to go alone or as the leader of a group of young women to confront Attila. She also prophesied that the town would be spared from destruction.

After rallying the Parisians, Geneviève met with Attila at the walls of the town, and according to the legend, she convinced him to spare the city. The story of her brave act spread and became a symbol of courage for those who resisted the Huns. Geneviève was later named a saint by the Catholic Church and today is the patron saint of Paris.

Because she saved the city from Attila, St. Geneviève is patron saint of Paris.

it and killing its population. Gregory of Tours wrote that the only building that was not destroyed was the oratory of the deacon, Stephen, who had prayed to the apostles that it might be spared. According to the account, he had a vision in which the oratory would be spared but the city would be destroyed because of the sins of its inhabitants.

It was during this time that Attila began to be called the "Scourge of God," a title that has stuck to him through the ages. The Christian historians of the time believed that Attila was God's instrument to punish and destroy towns and people that had fallen into sinful ways. Only divine protection through the intervention of saints or bishops or the righteous behavior of its citizens would allow a city to be spared.

Attila's army next marched toward Paris, which the Romans called Lutetia, destroying every town along the way. At the time, Lutetia was a strategically insignificant small town located on an island in the Seine River. Attila's army did not attack the town, possibly because other larger cities had greater riches to plunder. He marched his army south toward Aurelianum, now known as Orleans, a city on the Loire River about eighty miles away. The Hun army advanced without encountering resistance from the Romans.

Aurelianum

In the meantime, Aëtius had delayed in setting forth from Italy. The size of his army had been reduced by a famine, but as he traveled toward Gaul in late April, he made an alliance with the Visigoths, a large Christian barbarian group that had taken control of much of southern Gaul. Led by King Theodoric, they were a formidable fighting force that disliked the Huns because Attila's uncle Ruga had forced them out of Pannonia at the end of the fourth century. Another reason they allied themselves with the Romans was their fear that Attila's army would destroy their churches. The alliance worked to the Romans' advantage because Theodoric's decision persuaded soldiers from nearby clans to join their army, creating a force that equaled that of Attila. The large combined force of Romans, Visigoths, and allied barbarians also headed for the heavily fortified city of Aurelianum, in the hopes of seizing it before Attila's troops arrived.

In May 451 Attila and his army finally reached the city and laid siege to it. Setting up their battering rams against the city's walls, they began a fierce attack. The townspeople resisted by shooting volleys of arrows and pouring hot oil on the invaders. Suddenly, in early June, Aëtius and his large army appeared. Attila was taken by surprise because he did not know that the Romans and Visigoths had joined forces.

In the face of this large force, Attila consulted his shamans, who examined the entrails of cattle and scraped bones to foresee the future. The seers predicted a defeat for the Huns and also prophesied that the leader of the opposing army, presumably Aëtius, would be killed in the battle. The possibility of defeat was a new experience for Attila, who had become confident that his army could force any city to surrender. Fearing that his army could be trapped in a confrontation with the Roman force inside the city walls of Aurelianum, he decided not to attack the town at that time. He stopped the siege and withdrew his troops one hundred miles to the east, where they regrouped on the Catalaunian Plains near the town of Châlons. The Romans pursued them. Although the exact site is not known, historians believe the confrontation that followed occurred between the towns of Châlons and Troyes.

The Battle at Châlons

Attila knew that he would eventually have to face the large Roman army commanded by Aëtius, so he tried to choose a favorable location for the fight, preferably an open plain where he could use his mounted horsemen to their best advantage. Aware that the upcoming battle would involve defensive tactics as well as the offensive ones traditionally used by the Huns, who relied on lightning attacks, retreats, and then renewed attacks, he had his men dig trenches and set up a protective wall using their wagons.

On June 20, 451, the two forces faced one another, ready to attack. Before the battle began, Attila addressed his army in a speech, which was later described by the historian Jordanes. He said,

> Here you stand after conquering mighty nations and subduing the world. I therefore think it foolish for me to goad [encourage] you with words, as though you were men who had not been proved in action. . . . Seek swift victory in that spot where the battle rages, for when the sinews are cut the limbs soon relax, nor can a body stand when you have taken away the bones. Let your courage rise and your own fury burst forth.[34]

Ready for combat, the Huns attacked the Romans around nine o'clock in the morning.

The Battle Begins

As the battle began, Attila's army shot a huge volley of arrows at the Romans, and the Huns charging on horseback gained an initial advantage, breaking through the middle of the Roman lines. Attila placed his most dependable Hunnic troops in the center of his line, with his Germanic allies on the right and the Ostrogoths on the left. Aëtius countered by placing the Alani, his weakest troops, in the center of his line to bear the brunt of the Huns' attack. He positioned his own Roman warriors on the left. The fierce Visigoths, commanded by Theodoric, made up the right side of the line. The hand-to-hand fighting that followed was extremely bloody. Jordanes wrote that a stream was turned into a

The Roman Army

In the fourth century the Romans relied on a large army to protect the boundaries of the empire from the barbarians. The exact number of men in the armed forces is unknown, but a sixth-century source lists approximately 435,000 fighters. The land forces were made up of mobile field armies and guards who were stationed at frontier forts. These fortresses, spaced at regular intervals along the borders of the empire, were used to observe suspicious movements of barbarian forces.

Most of the men in the Roman army were in the infantry, but there were also cavalry units made up of horsemen who could rapidly move from place to place. By the fifth century, the importance of the cavalry had grown as a response to Attila's mounted warriors.

The Romans employed mercenary barbarians, including Huns, who fought in units made up of their own tribes and commanded by their own chieftains. Although the army was composed of diverse soldiers, the overall command and decisions were made by professional generals.

Because the greatest threat to the empire was from the barbarians to the north, the navy did not have the same importance as the army. However, flotillas of small ships sailed on the larger rivers such as the Rhine and the Danube and played a role in the defense of the empire.

A Roman soldier is depicted in this mosaic from Constantinople.

river of blood and those who were thirsty drank water mixed with gore.

As the Huns drove through the center of the Roman line, Theodoric urged his men to attack on the side flank. At some point in the battle he was thrown from his horse and killed, fulfilling the prediction of Attila's seers that one of the leaders on the Roman side would die in battle. His son Thorismund took over command of the Visigoth troops, who attacked the Huns with vengeance. In the fighting that followed Attila was almost killed.

During the first day of fighting the Roman-Visigoth army gained an advantage over the Huns. As night fell Attila retreated to the protection of his encampment. Because Attila's worst fear was being captured by the Romans, he ordered his men to make a large pile of wooden saddles and other cavalry equipment that would be set on fire if capture seemed imminent. He would throw himself on this burning pyre to avoid being taken alive by the Romans. Through the night the Huns protected their defensive position by shooting arrows at the enemy.

The next morning the Romans awoke to a battlefield that was piled high with the bodies of fallen warriors from both sides. When they realized that the Huns were not coming out of their encampment to continue the fighting, they were perplexed. Jordanes reported that the Romans "knew that Attila would not flee from battle unless overwhelmed by a great disaster. Yet he did nothing cowardly, like one that is overcome, but with clash of arms sounded the trumpets and threatened an attack."[35]

The Battle Is Indecisive

Seeing that his army had an advantage over the Huns, Aëtius held a council of war with his allies. The Visigoths, seeking revenge for the death of their king, were eager to continue fighting. Finally, they decided to surround Attila's encampment so that supplies could not be brought in. This strategy might have worked because Attila's army required a huge amount of food for both the soldiers and their animals, but the plan was not carried out. Instead, Aëtius unexpectedly withdrew his forces, ending the confrontation.

The reasons for his decision are unclear. Historians speculate that Aëtius wanted to maintain the balance of power within the Roman Empire. The complete destruction of the Huns might give too much power to other rival barbarians in the region. Perhaps he felt that he could use his diplomatic skills to negotiate with Attila as he had in the past. In prior years, the Huns had served the Romans as mercenary soldiers, and perhaps Aëtius wanted to keep this option open. Whatever the reason, rather than resuming the attack against the Huns, Aëtius urged Thorismund to return home to assert his power as new king of the Visigoths. The Romans then withdrew from the bloody battlefield. In

Attila, center, weighs his options in this painting of the Battle of Châlons. Some say he was defeated but the battle ended indecisively.

spite of the bloodshed, in which as many as 160,000 men had been killed, the results of the conflict were indecisive.

Attila Retreats

When Aëtius pulled back his Roman troops, Attila was confused, and he wondered if this was a strategy to force him into another attack. When a subsequent attack did not occur, he also turned his army around and retreated.

It is possible that his decision not to regroup to attack the Romans again was motivated by his concern that he might lose the fight.

Although those who were against Attila claimed that he had been defeated, the battle was not a definite victory for either the Romans or the Huns. The fight did have several important consequences, however. The Romans returned home with a significantly weakened force. Attila was stopped from moving deeper into the Roman territories of the north. The Visigoths, who had been a threat to both Rome and the Huns, were so weakened by their losses that they no longer were a major power in Gaul. And another northern group, the Franks, came to dominate the region, eventually giving their name to France.

Historians still argue about Attila's reasons for invading Gaul and subjecting his army to such a disastrous battle. Some believe that his motivation was a desire to find new territories to loot for goods to support his economy. It is possible that he wanted to gain control over new territory. Up to this time, his army of Huns had usually been victorious. Not winning a decisive victory against the western Romans would have been disappointing. At any rate, once home, Attila planned a way to seek revenge for the inconclusive outcome at the Battle of Châlons.

Chapter Six

ATTILA ATTACKS ITALY

For the first time in Attila's career as leader of the Huns, he had been forced to return to Pannonia without a definite victory. It is possible that the unsuccessful invasion of Gaul made him question his invincibility, but he had not lost his dreams of conquest. He knew that regaining his confidence and asserting his leadership over the Huns would require a decisive action in the months ahead. As French historian Marcel Brion writes, "Conquest based on ambition and greed can only be kept alive through incessant victories."[36]

The Return to Pannonia

The actions of Attila's army during its return to Pannonia contributed to the Huns' reputation as merciless aggressors. As they passed through territories that had not been touched by the warfare,

Attila's soldiers committed acts of terror, probably to vent their frustration about Châlons. According to historian Edward Gibbon, "They massacred their hostages as well as their captives; two hundred young maidens were torn asunder by wild horses, or their bones were crushed under the weight of rolling waggons; and their unburied limbs were abandoned on the public roads as a prey to dogs."[37]

When the army finally returned home in the winter, Attila took stock of his assets and planned his next moves. Although his enemies were spreading the news of his defeat on the Catalaunian Plains, Attila's army was still a powerful, loyal fighting force. During the winter he had time to analyze the reasons why the previous campaign had not been successful. He had observed the effectiveness of the Roman method

A skilled horseman, Attila prepares for battle in this painting. Until he failed to conquer Gaul, he believed himself invincible.

of fighting in which legions of armored men, many on foot, attacked as a mass.

Attila also noted the need to develop new machines of war. Brion writes, "Facing fortified towns he had seen the necessity for methods of attack such as the use of catapults. He had learned a different strategy of warfare, one that waged a wise, precise, and meticulous war."[38] To make his army more effective, he ordered them to practice new maneuvers, especially in the art of the siege, and he ordered that new battering rams and other armaments be built.

As the year wore on, Attila was faced with a lack of funds needed to maintain his economy and support the army. His successful attacks in the past had brought wealth to his kingdom, but his standoff with the Romans in Gaul had produced no spoils and his treasury was depleted. To remedy this, he demanded immediate payment of the usual yearly tribute from the Eastern Roman Empire, threatening war if he was refused.

Soldiers launch an attack with a catapult. Attila was quick to see the advantages of such war machines.

Marcian's Response

In Constantinople, meanwhile, Marcian had begun to assert his strength as a leader. Although he refused to deliver the annual tribute, he did agree to send a delegation under the command of an important ambassador named Apollonius to Attila's court to discuss relations between the Romans and the Huns. The delegation brought valuable gifts for the Huns. When Attila learned that the delegation was not bringing the tribute money, however, he angrily refused to meet them unless they handed over the emperor's gifts, threatening Apollonius with death if he refused. The ambassador replied that he would do so only if he were properly received by the Huns. If they killed him, the Romans' valuable presents would be considered spoils of war taken from a dead man. Angered by this response, Attila refused to let the ambassador and his delegation cross the Danube River into Pannonia, and Apollonius returned to Constantinople.

The relations between Attila and Marcian were in shambles. Because Attila was not sure that an attack on Constantinople would be successful at that time, he reconsidered his earlier threat and began to look at the possibility of invading Italy. Spring, the traditional time to start a campaign, was approaching, and his men were eager to return to battle. When he learned that Aëtius had returned to Italy with only a small number of his formerly large army, making the western empire a vulnerable target,

he made his decision. The Huns would attack Italy.

Attila's Motivation

Several factors explain Attila's decision to attack the Western Roman Empire. Most importantly, attacking Rome would allow him to acquire new plunder to help shore up his economy. Moreover, Attila apparently still planned to marry Honoria and wanted to again exert his demands for half of the Roman Empire as her dowry. In the spring of 452 he had sent a delegation to Rome to demand both Honoria and her dowry, a request that the Romans denied.

The desire for vengeance also played a role. Attila wanted revenge against the western Romans for his forced retreat the previous year in Gaul. He seemed to feel little gratitude toward Aëtius for his decision to stop the battle and spare him the humiliation of total defeat. According to some historians, by this time he had begun to hate his former friend.

Attila may also have believed that invading Italy would be easy. The Romans' alliance with the Visigoths had broken down, and the Romans had a smaller and weaker army than they had the year before in Gaul. Attila believed if he could first conquer the western Romans, then he could take on his other enemies, the eastern Romans and the Visigoths.

Some scholars also suggest that Attila may have thought that conquering Rome would be a stepping stone to con-

Attila and his Huns wreak havoc on the battlefield. Attila aspired to the conquest of Rome.

quering even greater territories. Because the once powerful Roman Empire had now weakened, defeating it was not an impossible dream. Earlier, another barbarian, Alaric, the king of the Visigoths, had attacked Rome three times, finally capturing and looting the city in 410.

In the spring of 452 Attila's army left Pannonia for northern Italy. Though the army was huge, perhaps as many as 100,000 men, it was smaller than the force he had gathered the previous year. Attila believed that a smaller, highly trained army would be more effective against the Romans than a larger, unmanageable force. The army, which was made up of Huns and warriors from allied Germanic barbarian tribes, moved across the Julian Alps and easily invaded northern Italy without any resistance.

Aëtius was totally unprepared for the Huns' invasion and had not stationed any troops in the Alps to stop their advance. Writes E.A. Thompson, "Attila crossed entirely without opposition, and the news of his arrival in Italy must have struck the patrician [Aëtius] with the violence of a thunderbolt."[39]

The Siege of Aquileia

Attila's army moved across the plains of northern Italy to the town of Aquileia, the strategic center of Rome's defense on its northeastern border. In addition to being a military center, it was also an important commercial hub and was at one time the only city other than Rome that could mint coins. Its location meant that whoever controlled it would also control northern Italy. The city was heavily fortified, and the Natisone River contributed to its defenses. The Romans believed that Aquileia's location and fortifications made it so strong that the town could not be defeated. The city had been placed under siege before, but it had never been forced to surrender. Even Alaric and his Visigoth army, who had conquered Rome in 410, had bypassed the town.

Because of Aquileia's importance as a gateway to the rest of Italy, Attila was determined to conquer it, and he ordered the army to lay siege. To his surprise, the town put up a strong resistance. The Huns were beaten back when they tried to attack the city walls, forcing Attila to send for reinforcements. After three months passed without success, Attila began to consider a retreat. His army was suffering from a lack of supplies, and little food was to be had in the surrounding countryside because famine had spread across Italy. Finally, he ordered his men to retreat the following day at sunrise.

A Strange Turn of Events

Just as the Huns were preparing to leave, a strange incident occurred. According to the Roman historian Procopius:

The following day about sunrise the barbarians had raised the siege and were already beginning their departure when a single male stork which had a nest on a certain tower

Aquileia

The town of Aquileia, which was destroyed by Attila in 452, is today a major archaeological site in Italy. Located on the Plain of Fruili near the Adriatic Sea, Aquileia was founded in the second century as a fortress city to protect the Italian peninsula against invasions of barbarians who lived north of the Alps mountain range. It was also a center of Roman culture and wealth and was one of the few Roman cities to have its own mint to manufacture coins. Before its destruction, Aquileia was a gateway for imports and artisans from the East and was home to a major Jewish community, many of whom were artists and merchants.

After the city was destroyed by Attila and his army, many of its surviving residents fled to nearby lagoons, where their community became the foundations of the city of Venice. Aquileia was eventually rebuilt, but it was destroyed again in 590 by the Lombards, who were Germanic invaders. It was rebuilt again, and was an important religious city during the Middle Ages.

Although Attila's army destroyed most of Aquileia, some objects remained, giving modern-day scholars insight into the lifestyle of those who lived in the town at the time of his invasion. Some of these objects are carved glass, pottery, coins, and sculptures, which are displayed at the National Archaeological Museum of Aquileia.

Aquileia was home to a Roman mint. This carving shows a workman minting coins.

A painting portrays Attila pointing at storks leaving the city of Aquileia. Attila saw this event as an omen of the city's fall and victory for the Huns.

of the city wall and was raising nestlings there, suddenly rose and left the place with his young. The father stork was flying, but the little storks, since they were not yet quite ready to fly, were at times sharing their father's flight and at times riding on his back, and thus they flew off and went away from the city.[40]

Attila, believing that this event was an omen that predicted the city would fall, ordered his men to resume their attack. A short time later, the part of the wall that had held the stork's nest fell, and the Huns poured into Aquileia and totally destroyed it. Most of the residents were massacred or taken as slaves; the few who managed to escape fled to several small islands nearby.

Valentinian

Flavius Valentinianus, who later became Valentinian III, ruler of the Western Roman Empire, was born in 419. When his mother, Galla Placidia, fell from favor with the Roman court, she and Valentinian, along with his sister Honoria, went into exile at the court of Theodosius II in Constantinople. The throne of the western empire was then grabbed by a rival named John who proclaimed himself emperor. After eighteen months on the throne, he was killed by forces loyal to Valentinian's mother, and Valentinian, then six years old, was declared emperor.

Valentinian was a weak monarch who relied on the advice of others. For much of his life he was overshadowed by his mother. Aëtius, his general, also wielded much power behind the throne. Although Valentinian relied on Aëtius's military skill, he distrusted him and considered him a rival. Jealous of his general's power, a year after Attila's death, Valentinian stabbed Aëtius to death. The next year, Valentinian himself was murdered by two of his bodyguards who were loyal to Aëtius.

Valentinian III was a weak emperor, easily dominated by advisors and others.

The news of the destruction of Aquileia spread terror throughout northern Italy, and city after city surrendered to the Huns hoping to escape similar devastation. Concordia, Altinum, and Verona were burned to the ground and their residents made slaves. Some cities that agreed to pay tribute to the Huns, however, were spared. Destroying a major town at the beginning of a military campaign to soften resistance was a strategy that Attila had used before. The siege of Metz the previous year had been intended to intimidate his opponents.

Forging on, the Huns conquered Mediolanum, now known as Milan, one of the most important cities in northern Italy. Because Mediolanum had served as a capital of the Roman Empire a hundred years earlier, the defeat of the city was a psychological blow to the Romans. For a short time Attila took up residence in the royal palace. While there he ordered a local artist to repaint a large mural depicting the Roman emperors of the east and west seated on their thrones. To demean the Romans, the altered painting showed a victorious Attila seated on a throne, looking down on the Roman leaders, who poured gold at his feet.

Aëtius's Response

Up to this point the Huns had not met with resistance from the Romans. Without the help of their allies, the Alani and the Visigoths, the Romans had been unable to mount a large army to resist Attila's forces. In the past, the Romans had largely depended on foreign mercenary soldiers, rather than their own citizens, to man their army. This practice contributed to their weakness.

Although Aëtius believed that the Romans should make a stand against the Huns, the emperor Valentinian disagreed, possibly because he disliked Aëtius and considered him a rival for power. Rather than staying put and fighting the invaders, the emperor decided to leave Ravenna and flee south to Rome, which was farther away from Attila's army. The emperor's religious convictions also played a role in his decision. Valentinian was a devout Christian, and some historians believe that he went to Rome to seek assistance from Pope Leo I, who resided in the city.

In the meantime, Attila and his army moved toward Ticinum, now known as Pavia, and then proceeded toward the Mincio River near the town of Mantua. Rather than continuing directly toward Rome, Attila's troops moved across the country in a haphazard manner. There are probably several reasons why they did not march directly to Rome. For one, his troops were running out of supplies for both men and the animals that accompanied the army. Marcel Brion writes, "The Huns found before them a ravaged country where no fruit or grain remained."[41] Illness was another reason for the army's hesitation. Apparently Attila's army was struck by an epidemic, possibly malaria, soon after leaving Milan.

An engraving shows Attila (left) meeting with Pope Leo I. According to legend, the pope persuaded Attila not to invade Rome.

Moreover, summer heat had spoiled food, causing diarrhea and dysentery.

Aëtius, meanwhile, had finally gathered a force to defend central Italy. In addition to Roman soldiers, his army included men sent by Marcian, the eastern emperor. Believing that Attila's absence had created vulnerability in the Hun's homeland, Marcian also sent a military force across the Danube into Pannonia. Attila was now faced with the possibility of fighting on two fronts, one in Italy and one in Pannonia. As he pondered whether to return to Pannonia, his troops neared Rome. His advisers urged him not to attack the city, reminding him that the Visigoth king Alaric had died soon after he had conquered Rome in 410. While Attila weighed their advice against his own desires to conquer the city, the Romans, fearing an immediate attack, sent a message to him asking for a meeting.

Pope Leo Intercedes

Even though Rome was no longer the capital of the Western Roman Empire, it was still an important city because it was the center of Christianity. Rome also had a psychological importance to the Romans because it symbolized their past glory as the most important power in the ancient world. They were determined not to let the city fall to Attila.

Archaeology

Because the Huns were nomads, they left very few remnants of their culture. The largest number of artifacts come from tombs located in Russia, Mongolia, and central Asia. Like other ancient peoples, the Huns and their predecessors placed valuables in the tombs of important people. Russian archaeologists who have excavated these sites have discovered bronze cauldrons, arms, and gold jewelry such as small stamped gold plaques that were sewn onto clothing and gold buckles. They believe that the bronze belts that were found in some of the tombs may have indicated their owners' rank and social position.

Although fewer objects remain from Attila's empire, artifacts belonging to his armies have been found in western Europe. Among the objects that probably came from Attila's army are large bronze pots, one of which is in the Hungarian National Museum in Budapest. Other finds include gold jewelry discovered in the vicinity of Szeged, Hungary, near the site of Attila's community. Although some gold items are on display at the Szeged Museum, it is believed that these are but a small part of the gold that once belonged to the Huns.

The historic meeting between Attila and the Romans took place on the shores of the Muncio River near the modern town of Verona. The Romans, knowing that Attila would expect a delegation of influential, important men, sent their most powerful diplomats. Trygetius, the prefect of Rome, was a skilled negotiator and a senator. Fifteen years earlier he had negotiated favorable terms with the Vandal king Geiseric. Aveinus was a wealthy, important politician. The third member of the delegation was Pope Leo, the head of the Catholic Church. Leo, later known as Leo the Great, was a dynamic man with great faith and administrative skills. The goal of the delegation was to persuade Attila to stay away from Rome. To impress Attila with their importance, the diplomats dressed in a manner that showed their high rank. Leo wore crimson robes and a miter made of silk embroidered with gold.

Attila received the delegation in his tent on July 6, 452. To show that he was not awed by their importance, he did not rise to meet them but reclined on his couch while he listened to their requests. Although he was unintimidated by their importance, he seemed to be impressed by Leo's magnificent garments and bearing. At first Attila was unsympathetic to their requests, but according to Hungarian legend, during the negotiations he was swayed by a vision in which he met two of the founders of the Christian faith, St. Peter and St. Paul, who told him not to attack Rome. They said that God no longer wanted him to be a scourge or instrument to punish the wicked by destroying their cities and that he would die instantly if he did not agree to retreat.

Attila did agree to spare Rome, and a short time later he returned to Pannonia. Prosper, a Christian historian writing in 455 about the historic meeting between Leo and Attila, credits the pope with convincing Attila to give up his plan to conquer Rome. The significance of Leo's intervention has been debated by historians, many of whom believe that Attila was more influenced by the lack of food in Italy and the weakening of his troops by illness than by the pleas of the Roman delegation. Some scholars also believe that he was following his customary pattern of waging war for plunder in the summer and then returning to Pannonia before winter set in, which would make the return trip across the Alps dangerous and difficult.

No matter what Attila's reasons for giving up his plan to attack Rome, the venture had been successful for him because the Romans had agreed to pay him a large tribute in gold. They also gave him the important title of *magister militium*, or commander in chief. Once he had led his troops safely back to their homeland to spend the winter, however, Attila again demanded that Honoria be sent to him as a bride, hinting that if the Romans refused, they would face renewed hostilities in the future.

Although his invasion of Italy in 452 had not resulted in adding new

Chapter Seven

Attila's Death and the Decline of the Huns

Attila's invasion of Italy had not resulted in a victory over the western Romans, but he was still one of the most powerful men in Europe. His empire spread over a large portion of central Europe, and his name caused fear in the territories he had not yet conquered. In the seven years of his reign his army had destroyed over a hundred cities, killed thousands of people, and extorted a huge amount of gold from both the Eastern and Western Roman empires. After he returned to Pannonia in 452, he weighed the best actions to take to continue his aggression and to ensure a steady flow of plunder into his treasury.

His attention turned toward the eastern empire, which had once again refused to pay him the agreed-upon tribute in gold. The Goth historian Jordanes wrote, "Attila returned to his own country, seeming to regret the peace and vexed at the cessation of war. For he sent ambassadors to Marcian, Emperor of the East, threatening to devastate the provinces because that which had been promised to him . . . was in no wise performed, and saying that he would show himself more cruel to his foes than ever."[42]

Attila announced to his men that they would attack the eastern empire in the spring. It is possible that he actually planned to attack the eastern empire, but instead he changed his mind. His next move was a crafty and shrewd decision designed to keep his enemies off balance.

Attila Again Attacks the West

Rather than taking action against the eastern empire, in early 453 Attila moved his army to the west to attack the

The Huns attack the Alani in Gaul, another of Attila's failed attempts to conquer Gaul.

Alani, a barbarian tribe that had settled near the Loire River in Gaul. The settlements of the Alani were a buffer state between the lands controlled by the Huns and those of the Visigoths. Defeating the Alani would open the way for an attack against the Visigoths, whom the Huns hated because of their alliance with the Romans during the Battle of Châlons. A victory would also contribute to Attila's dream of adding territories west of the Rhine River to his empire.

Attila moved his troops toward Gaul, where they attacked the Alani. Jordanes wrote of the battle; however, he did not give the location of the encounter. He wrote that Thorismund, the new king of the Visigoths, "with quickness of thought, perceived Attila's trick. By forced marches he came to the Alani before him [Attila] and was well prepared to check the advance of Attila when he came after him. They joined battle in almost the same way as before at the Catalaunian Plains, and Thorismund dashed his hopes of victory, for he routed him and drove him from the land without a triumph, compelling him to flee to his own country."[43]

After his foray into Gaul failed, Attila retreated and headed back to Pannonia. Some historians believe that as he passed through lands belonging to his Germanic vassals, he disciplined barbarian tribes who had tried to proclaim their independence from the Huns by executing their chieftains.

Ildico

By the spring of 453 Attila had safely returned home and was planning to take a new wife, named Ildico. Little is known about his bride except that she was young and beautiful. Some scholars speculate that she was the daughter of one of the chiefs he had killed, perhaps of the Burgundians, a Germanic tribe that had settled in what is now southeastern France.

His reasons for entering into a new marriage at this time are unclear. There was a great age discrepancy between the two. By now Attila was in his mid-fifties, and Ildico was about sixteen. Because polygamy was an accepted practice among the Huns, he already had a large number of wives and many children. Perhaps the marriage was made for political reasons; however, it is also possible that Attila was infatuated by her beauty.

The wedding, which took place at Attila's wooden palace on the Tisza River, was a festive event. In attendance were Attila's vassals, slaves, and a throng of loyal supporters. Marcel Brion writes, "The tribal chiefs had brought gifts such as horses, mare's milk in wooden vessels, jewels of gold and jade, purple fabrics, tapestries, embroidered silks and saddles encrusted with precious stones."[44] Eating and drinking went on through the night. According to custom, Attila toasted and drank to the health of each of his guests. By the time he and his bride retired to their bedchamber after midnight, he was weakened by drink and sleepiness. The servants knew better than to disturb them.

The next day Attila's friends and attendants became concerned when he had not appeared by noon. Finally, his friend Edeco ordered the servants to break down the door of the bedchamber. According to Priscus, "They found Attila dead from a flow of blood, unwounded, and the girl with [a] downcast look weeping beneath her veil."[45] At first Attila's followers believed that Ildico had murdered their leader, but finding no wounds, they eventually accepted that he had probably suffocated from a massive nosebleed.

To show their grief, the Huns disfigured themselves. Priscus explains: "As is the custom of that race, they cut off part of their hair and disfigured their faces horribly with deep wounds so that the distinguished warrior might be bewailed, not with feminine lamentations and tears, but with manly blood."[46] The news of Attila's death soon reached the Romans,

Attila's attendants discover him dead in bed and his new bride weeping. He is thought to have died of a massive hemorrhage.

who were delighted that their archenemy was dead.

Although Attila's death was probably the result of a hemorrhage caused by drinking too much alcohol at the wedding celebration, speculation about his death circulated throughout the Roman world. The Roman historian Ammianus Marcellinus wrote that he had been stabbed in the night by a woman. Another rumor suggested that there had been a political conspiracy to assassinate Attila, a plot allegedly carried out by his trusted friends Orestes and Edeco, who may have been bribed by Marcian. Around the same time as Attila's death, it was reported that Marcian had a dream in which he saw Attila's broken bow, a sign that his enemy had died.

Attila's Funeral

Attila was buried with much pomp. After his body was laid out under a silk canopy in the center of a plain for all to see, the most important Hunnic horsemen galloped around it. A funeral hymn

The Legend of Attila in Literature and Opera

Attila has lived on as a central figure in literature and opera, and his character has been depicted in various ways. In the Middle Ages he was portrayed as the scourge of God and the enemy of the human race. In the ninth century he appeared in Nordic legends with the name Atli, Atla, or Etzel. In the "Song of Attila," an epic narrative poem from medieval Germany, he is a taciturn and dark character who kills Gunthar, the king of Burgundy, and marries his wife, Kremhilda. In the German legend of the Nibelungen, however, Attila, named Etzel, merges as a wise, considerate, middle-aged man.

During the Renaissance, Attila was the protagonist of several Italian, French, and Spanish dramas and plays. The seventeenth-century French playwright Corneille transformed Attila into a melodramatic king who worried about public hatred. In the opera *Attila* by Guiseppe Verde, written in the 1840s, the action begins during the Huns' devastation of Aquileia, when Attila takes Odabella (Ildico) captive. Attila is then turned away from the gates of Rome by Pope Leo. Later, after Attila has married Odabella, she stabs him to death in the presence of Ezio (Aëtius). The opera was written at a time when Italy was struggling for independence and unification. Although the story had no connection with current events, it was filled with conspiracies, assassinations, and appeals to liberty that resonated with the Italian public.

told of Attila's life and accomplishments. The song states:

> Chief of the Huns, King Attila, born of Mundzuk his father, lord of the mightiest races, who alone, with power unknown before his time, held the Scythian and German realms and even terrified both empires of the Roman world, captured their cities, and . . . took yearly tribute from them to save the rest from being plundered. When he had done all these things through the kindness of fortune, neither by an enemy's wound nor a friend's treachery but with his nation secure, amid his pleasures, and in happiness and without a sense of pain he fell.[47]

Attila's male followers then placed his body in three coffins, the first made of gold, the second made of silver, and the third made of iron. Priscus explained that the iron symbolized the peoples he had subdued, and the gold and silver indicated the honors he had received from both the Eastern and Western Roman empires. They also added weapons taken from those they had conquered, along with jewels and ornaments that indicated his royal position. To keep his burial place secret, those who had assisted in preparing the body were slaughtered. As Jordanes wrote, "Thus sudden death was the lot of those who buried him as well as of him who was buried."[48]

The burial site has never been discovered, but some archaeologists believe that it may be located somewhere between the Tisza and Danube rivers in an area that covers more than thirteen thousand square miles of modern-day Yugoslavia. According to a Hungarian legend, his body was buried beneath the Tisza River to make it difficult for tomb robbers to loot it. Because the coffin was probably not inscribed with Attila's name, if found it will be difficult to identify.

The Huns After Attila's Death

After Attila's funeral rites were over, bickering broke out among Attila's sons over who would lead the Huns. One of Attila's greatest shortcomings as a leader was that he had not planned for the continuation of rule after his death. Although he had many children (as many as sixty according to some accounts), only Ellak, Dengizik, and Ernak, his sons by his principal wife, Kreka, had the right of succession. Immediately after his burial, Ellak, the eldest son, succeeded his father as king. His position was supported by Attila's chief lieutenant, Onegesius. Their idea was to maintain the system of absolute control that Attila had developed.

Ellak's two younger brothers objected to this arrangement. Dengizik and Attila's favorite son, Ernak, wanted to divide their father's kingdom much like it had been when Attila and Bleda had shared the kingship. To pacify them, it

Atlantic
Ocean

SCANDINAVIA

North
Sea

Baltic Sea

BRITANNIA

Rhine

GERMANIA

E U R O P E

Volga

451

370

Battle of
Chålons

Paris •

×

Danube

GAUL

PANNONIA

Tisza R.

• Toulouse

Venice
Ravenna

Aquileia

Black Sea

SPAIN

450

Adriatic Sea

ITALY

395

420

Rome •

GREECE

Constantinople •

ASIA MINOR   ASSYRIA

Mediterranean Sea

EGYPT

Nile

A F R I C A

**The Empire of
Attila the Hun
450 A.D.**

370 ⟵ Hun's invasion
route and year

was decided to give them control over several of the groups who worked for the Huns as soldiers or as farmers.

Dividing the vast kingdom into separate parts under three different leaders led to instability, and within a year fighting began between factions supporting different brothers. Ellak was able to resolve the conflict in the area he controlled. Dengizik and Ernak, meanwhile, were forced to flee for their own safety to areas of the Hunnic territory not under their brother's command.

The resulting instability created an opportunity for rebellion among some of the tribes that had owed allegiance to Attila. Ellak faced an uprising in the north among the Gepids, a tribe that had always been loyal to Attila and that had fought with him during his foreign battles. They were encouraged in their rebellion by Marcian, who believed that dividing the Huns' empire was a way to weaken them as an adversary. In 454, a year after Attila's death, the Gepids fought a decisive battle with the Huns near the Nedao River in Pannonia. The Huns were defeated, and Ellak was killed. The Gepids took control of a large part of the territory between the Danube and Tisza rivers, including the area where the Huns' capital was located. This was the beginning of the dissolution of Attila's empire.

The Decline of the Huns

The Gepids' victory pushed Ernak, Dengizik, and their followers to an area of the lower Danube, where over the next ten years they tried to develop a new

The Hungarian View of Attila

In western Europe Attila is considered a cruel aggressor, but in Hungary he is viewed as a heroic figure. A cult around his life and deeds arose during the reign of King Matthias Corvinus, who ruled from 1458 to 1490. During this period Attila was described as a brave warrior and an enlightened leader, and many Hungarians bragged that they were descendants of Attila. Whenever Hungary was threatened by outside invaders, Attila's name was used as a rallying point for national pride.

In his biography *Attila, King of the Huns*, author Patrick Howarth writes, "Indeed, through all ages of Hungarian history Attila has been regarded with veneration, and his standing today is as high as it ever was .... In Hungary he is the enlightened ruler, the national hero." In modern Hungary, Attila is regarded as a popular folk hero. Boys are named after him, and one of the main streets in modern Budapest also bears his name. In 1993 the staging of a patriotic rock opera called *Attila* was a popular cultural event.

home for the Huns. In 466 they sent a delegation to Constantinople to Marcian's successor, Leo, to ask him to grant them a free market on the Danube where the Huns could barter and sell goods. They also apologized for the problems the Huns had caused in the past.

Because the Huns were no longer a military threat to his empire, Leo rejected their demands. Dengizik responded aggressively. In 466–467 he led an army across the Danube. He also sent another delegation to Leo demanding land and tribute and threatening war if his requests were not met. Leo again refused. The resulting war lasted two years and ended in a total defeat for the Huns. Dengizik was killed, and his skull was displayed in Constantinople as a symbol of retribution for all the trouble that the Huns had created for the empire during Attila's reign.

Ernak was less aggressive than his brother. When he asked Leo to grant his people land, the emperor gave him territory in the eastern section of Romania in an area called Transylvania. In the sixteen years that had passed since Attila's death, his once mighty Hun empire had fallen from power. Attila's name, however, would continue to be synonymous with evil.

Attila's Reputation

Attila was sole ruler of the Huns for only eight years, but during this brief time he gained a sinister reputation that has lasted for centuries. During his reign, he was a feared leader who threatened to conquer both the Eastern and Western Roman empires, and his conquests were a major factor in bringing about the fall of the Western Roman Empire in 476. His success was the result of his cruelty, greed, and arrogance, which caused terror among both the weaker barbarian tribes he came to dominate and the Romans he wished to conquer. Although the Romans' fears were justified, their prejudice against barbarians also contributed to Attila's bad reputation.

Historians believe that Attila's negative image was influenced by the Romans' belief that the Huns were subhuman beings whose lifestyle and customs were uncivilized. Even before Attila's birth, Roman chroniclers had written about the Huns' savage lifestyle. One Roman historian said they lived the life of animals. Jordanes wrote that they were "a race almost of man."[49] The pagan religion of the Huns and Attila, which included sacrificing animals and reliance on the advice of elders known as shamans, was looked down upon by the Christian Romans. The fact that Attila shunned Roman customs and persisted in his own traditions also contributed to his reputation as an uncultured barbarian.

Despite his fearsome reputation however, Attila was also known as a dynamic leader. Although he was an unscrupulous negotiator who used extortion as a way to gain wealth and power, he

Attila is portrayed here as a medieval king. The fabled Hun leader has inspired literature, operas, and even a modern style of business management.

The Leadership Secrets of the Huns

In the 1980s the book Leadership Secrets of Attila the Hun, *by Wess Roberts, caused a stir. The book combines a biography of Attila with some of his supposed ideas on leadership that might apply to modern business management. These principles include the following:*

A chieftain who asks the wrong questions always hears the wrong answers.

The greatness of a Hun is measured by the sacrifices he is willing to make for the good of the nation.

Great chieftains never take themselves too seriously.

Every decision involves some risk.

Huns only make enemies on purpose.

was also a talented commander who was able to unite many diverse barbarian tribes into a powerful fighting force that threatened the most powerful empire in the world at the time. That these men were intensely loyal to him attests to his leadership ability. In his best-selling book *Leadership Secrets of Attila the Hun*, author Wess Roberts writes, "Attila with his magnetic force, influence and perhaps charm, through which he united the Huns, was so awe inspiring to his warriors and chieftains that he was worshiped by them—even as a god by some."[50] His popularity among his own people was also partly due to the moderation he sometimes expressed in his behavior toward them. Priscus wrote that he was "personally restrained in action, most impressive in counsel, gracious to suppliants, and generous to those to whom he had once given his trust."[51]

Priscus, however, was also aware of the violent side of Attila's personality, which has contributed to his enduring villainous reputation. He wrote that Attila was "a man born to shake the races of the world, a terror to all lands, who in some way or other frightened everyone by the dread report noised abroad about him."[52] Attila's reputation as one of history's cruelest tyrants has lived on for centuries. He remains one of history's most intriguing characters.

NOTES

Chapter 1: Preparation for Leadership

1. Marcel Brion, *La Vie d'Attila* [The Life of Attila]. Paris: Librairie Gallimard, 1933, p. 28.
2. Quoted in Otto J. Maenchen-Helfen, *The World of the Huns*. Berkeley and Los Angeles: University of California Press, 1973, p. 251.
3. Brion, *La Vie d'Attila*, p. 31.
4. Brion, *La Vie d'Attila*, p. 31.
5. Brion, *La Vie d'Attila*, p. 35.
6. Brion, *La Vie d'Attila*, pp. 35–36.
7. Maenchen-Helfen, *The World of the Huns*, p. 86.
8. Maenchen-Helfen, *The World of the Huns*, p. 77.
9. Maenchen-Helfen, *The World of the Huns*, p. 86.
10. Patrick Howarth, *Attila, King of the Huns: The Man and the Myth*. New York: Carroll & Graff, 2001, p. 36.
11. Howarth, *Attila, King of the Huns*, p. 36.
12. Brion, *La Vie d'Attila*, p. 36.

Chapter 2: Attila Takes on the Role of Leader

13. Howarth, *Attila, King of the Huns*, p. 35.
14. E.A. Thompson, *The Huns*. Oxford, England: Blackwell, 1996, p. 85.
15. Brion, *La Vie d'Attila*, p. 51.

16. Quoted in Howarth, *Attila, King of the Huns*, p. 26.
17. Thompson, *The Huns*, p. 95.
18. Brion, *La Vie d'Attila*, p. 66.

Chapter 3: Attila's Conquests in the East

19. Quoted in Maenchen-Helfen, *The World of the Huns*, p. 279.
20. Colin Douglas Gordon, *The Age of Attila*. Ann Arbor: University of Michigan Press, 1960, p. 70.
21. Quoted in Maenchen-Helfen, *The World of the Huns*, p. 202.
22. Quoted in Thompson, *The Huns*, p. 103.
23. Quoted in Howarth, *Attila, King of the Huns*, p. 51.
24. Maenchen-Helfen, *The World of the Huns*, p. 124.
25. Maenchen-Helfen, *The World of the Huns*, p. 125.

Chapter 4: A Plot to Kill Attila

26. Thompson, *The Huns*, p. 116.
27. Thompson, *The Huns*, p. 119.
28. Quoted in Gordon, *The Age of Attila*, p. 84.
29. Quoted in Howarth, *Attila, King of the Huns*, pp. 73–74.
30. Quoted in Howarth, *Attila, King of the Huns*, p. 74.
31. Quoted in Howarth, *Attila, King of the Huns*, p. 76.

32. Howarth, *Attila, King of the Huns*, pp. 79–80.

Chapter 5: Attila Turns His Attention West
33. Quoted in Howarth, *Attila, King of the Huns*, p. 91.
34. Quoted in Howarth, *Attila, King of the Huns*, p. 109.
35. Quoted in *The Battle of Chalons, 451, CE*," *Medieval Sourcebook*, www.fordham.edu/halsall/source/451/jordanes/38.

Chapter 6: Attila Attacks Italy
36. Brion, *La Vie d'Attila*, pp. 201–202.
37. Quoted in Howarth, *Attila, King of the Huns*, p. 119.
38. Brion, *La Vie d'Attila*, p. 204.
39. Thompson, *The Huns*, p. 159.
40. Quoted in Howarth, *Attila, King of the Huns*, pp. 122–23.
41. Brion, *La Vie d'Attila*, p. 232.

Chapter 7: Attila's Death and the Decline of the Huns
42. Quoted in Howarth, *Attila, King of the Huns*, p. 137.
43. Quoted in Howarth, *Attila, King of the Huns*, pp. 38–39.
44. Brion, *La Vie d'Attila*, p. 248.
45. Quoted in Gordon, *The Age of Attila*, p. 110.
46. Quoted in Gordon, *The Age of Attila*, p. 110.
47. Quoted in Gordon, *The Age of Attila*, p. 111.
48. Quoted in Howarth, *Attila, King of the Huns*, p. 139.
49. Quoted in Thompson, *The Huns*, p. 11.
50. Wess Roberts, *Leadership Secrets of Attila the Hun*. New York: Warner, 1989, p. 60.
51. Quoted in Gordon, *The Age of Attila*, p. 61.
52. Quoted in Gordon, *The Age of Attila*, p. 61.

CHRONOLOGY

c. 374
Huns arrive in Europe from Central Asia.

c. 400
Attila is born.

401
Attila's father, Mundzuk, dies.

405
Aëtius, a young Roman, is sent as hostage to the Huns.

c. 408–410
Attila is sent as a hostage to the Roman court in Ravenna. Attila's grandfather, King Ruga, becomes the main ruler of the Huns.

425
Valentinian II becomes emperor of the Western Roman Empire.

434
Ruga dies. The kingship of the Huns is shared by Attila and his brother, Bleda.

435
The Treaty of Margus between Attila and Bleda and the eastern Romans requires the Romans to pay gold to the Huns to insure peace.

438–439
Attila leads campaigns to bring the Hunnic tribes of the Caucasus under the control of him and Bleda. The campaigns against the eastern empire begin.

440
Attila and Bleda begin a four-year war with the Eastern Roman Empire.

443
First Peace of Anatolius between the Huns and the eastern empire humiliates Constantinople.

444
Bleda dies. Attila takes control of the Hunnic Empire. The so-called Sword of God is discovered. Attila plans to create a world empire.

445–6
Attila attacks and conquers Balkans.

447
The Second Peace of Anatolius imposes harsh terms against Constantinople.

449
Theodosius II agrees to plot to assassinate Attila. The plot fails.

449
Priscus accompanies Roman delegation to Attila's capital for negotiations.

450
Theodosius dies and is succeeded by Marcian.

451
Attila invades Gaul (France). The Battle of Châlons between Aëtius and Attila results in the deaths of approximately 100,000 men. The battle is a draw.

452
Attila attacks Italy in March. He conquers and destroys twelve cities.

452
Pope Leo I convinces Attila to withdraw his troops from Italy.

453
Attila marries Ildico and dies on his wedding night.

454
Ellak, Attila's son and successor, dies.

469
Dengizik, Attila's son, dies after being defeated by Romans in Constantinople. The Hunnic empire disintegrates. Ernak, Attila's youngest son, takes remaining Huns to what is today Romania.

476
The Roman Empire falls to barbarians.

FOR FURTHER READING

Books

Bonnie Carman Harvey, *Attila the Hun*. Philadelphia: Chelsea House, 2003. This biography for teens includes many maps and illustrations about Attila's life and times.

Scott Ingram, *Attila the Hun*. San Diego: Blackbirch, 2002. This is a shorter biography of Attila documenting his life and villainous deeds.

David Matz, *Daily Life of the Ancient Romans*. Westport, CT: Greenwood, 2002. A social history about the customs and lifestyles of the ancient Romans.

Don Nardo, *The Roman Empire*. San Diego: Lucent, 1994. This book traces the rise of the Roman Empire from 60 B.C. to A.D. 1453 and deals with the history and customs of the empire.

Wess Roberts, *Leadership Secrets of Attila the Hun*. New York: Warner, 1987. Young readers will enjoy the descriptions of Attila's life and the leadership secrets he might have believed in.

Stephen Bela Vardy, *Attila*. New York: Chelsea House, 1991. A rather scholarly biography of the life of Attila

with interesting illustrations and quotes from other biographers.

Robert N. Webb, *Attila, King of the Huns*. New York: Franklin Watts, 1965. This descriptive biography about Attila reads like a novel.

Videos

Attila, Scourge of God. A&E Television Network, 1994. A fairly accurate rendition of Attila's life, this video shows many of the places where he lived and fought and gives viewers an idea of what life was like in the fifth century.

Web sites

Aquileia (www.aquileia.it). This official Web site of the town of Aquileia, which was destroyed by Attila, gives a virtual 3-D tour of some of the archaeological sites.

De Bellis Antiquitatis Resource Page (www.fanaticus.org/dba/battles/chalons.html). This site, a virtual community for ancient and medieval war gamers and history buffs, contains a detailed description of the Battle of Châlons.

Eyewitness to History (www.eyewitness

tohistory.com/attila.htm). This Web site includes Priscus's description of the banquet he attended as a guest of Attila and has a map of western Europe showing the routes Attila took to Châlons and Italy.

Internet Medieval Source Book (www. fordham.edu/halsall/sbook.html). This site, hosted by Fordham University, contains maps of the medieval period and a description of Attila's court by Priscus.

WORKS CONSULTED

Books

Marcel Brion, *La Vie d'Attila* [The Life of Attila]. Paris: Librairie Gallimard, 1993. This is a well-written, colorful French biography of Attila.

Philip Dixon, *Barbarian Europe*. Oxford, England: Elsevier, 1976. A lavishly illustrated book describing the barbarian cultures in western Europe; gives insights into the homes and lifestyles of various tribes.

Edward Gibbon, *The Decline and Fall of the Roman Empire*. New York: Modern Library, 2003. Originally published in the eighteenth century, this classic volume describes the conditions leading to the fall of the Roman Empire. Several chapters are dedicated to Attila and the Huns.

Colin Douglas Gordon, *The Age of Attila*. Ann Arbor: University of Michigan Press, 1960. This book includes translations from Latin of the impressions of the Greco-Roman historian Priscus.

Gerard Herzhaft, *Yo, Attila*. Madrid: Grupo Anaya, 1991. The Spanish translation of a work originally published in German, this book combines fiction and fact to present a first-person description of Attila's life and thoughts.

Patrick Howarth, *Attila, King of the Huns: The Man and the Myth*. New York: Carroll & Graf, 2001. Howarth's book describes the Huns, their culture, the life of Attila, and his impact on different European cultures.

Otto J. Maenchen-Helfen, *The World of the Huns*. Berkeley and Los Angeles: University of California Press, 1973. A description of the culture of the Huns before and during Attila's lifetime.

Pauline Stafford, *Queens, Concubines, and Dowagers: The King's Wife in the Early Middle Ages*. Athens: University of Georgia Press, 1983. Although this book does not deal specifically with the Huns, it gives insights into the lives of women in Europe in the Middle Ages.

E.A. Thompson, *The Huns*. Oxford, England: Blackwell, 1996. Thompson presents an interesting study of the lifestyles of the Huns and the life of Attila.

Internet Sources

Jordanes, "Deeds and Origins of the

Goths," trans. Charles C. Mierow. www.acs.ucalgar.ca/~vandersp/ courses/texts/jordgeti.html. Translation of Jordanes' sixth-century text about Attila and the Huns.

Priscus, "Priscus at the Court of Attila," trans. J.B. Bury. http://ccat.sas.upenn. edu/jod/texts/priscus.html. A translation of the Greco-Roman historian's visit to Attila's kingdom.

INDEX

PICTURE CREDITS

About
The Author

Marilyn Tower Oliver is the author of more than 275 articles for adults and children, which have appeared in national and regional publications such as *The Los Angeles Times*, *Dolls*, and *Valley Magazine*, where she is a contributing editor. She has also written eight books for young adults including *Natural Crafts*, *The Importance of Muhammad* (Lucent Books, 2003), and *The Importance of Henry VIII* (Lucent Books, 2004). She also produces and hosts a southern California cable television talk show about opera called *Opera! Opera! Opera!* Oliver is a distinguished graduate of Stanford University where she received a master of arts degree in secondary education. She is an accomplished silversmith as well. She lives in Los Angeles with a miniature poodle and a Siamese cat.